The Albert Memorial

Stephen Bayley

The Albert Memorial

The monument in its social and architectural context

Scolar Press   London

First published 1981 by
SCOLAR PRESS
James Price Publishing Ltd
13 Brunswick Centre
London WC1N 1AF

Paperback edition published 1983

British Library Cataloguing in Publication Data
    Bayley, Stephen
    The Albert Memorial
    1. London. Albert Memorial
    942.1'32   DA689.A/

ISBN 0 85967 674 9

Printed in Great Britain by
Whitstable Litho Ltd, Whitstable, Kent

Also by Stephen Bayley
IN GOOD SHAPE

Contents

List of Plates

Much of the source material used in the preparation of this book rests in the Royal Archives at Windsor, and was drawn on by gracious permission of Her Majesty The Queen

Acknowledgements

Cautious about leaving some good cameras in a car in a bad area of Islington, I entered subterranean N1 festooned with Nikons one night early in 1976. In the basement I met Paul Overy. He deserves the first acknowledgement here because when he found out that, for amusement alone, I had been taking photographs of the Albert Memorial he told me that he had been asked to write a book about it. He did not want to. Did I? I did. Paul Overy then introduced me to his agent John Johnson who, together with his successor, Andrew Hewson, acted throughout the long business of producing this book with degrees of charm and patience which seem almost eccentric in an unchivalrous world.

The substance of the book owes more to the competence and energy of others than it does to me. Prominent now must be the names of Jane Langton and Elizabeth Cuthbert, who administer The Royal Archives at Windsor, where most of the work on this book was done. For more than two summers I was locked in an *Almanach de Gotha* lined cell in The Round Tower at Windsor by these well-meaning ladies, emerging only when moved to despair by a palaeographical problem which one or other of them rapidly proved to be on every occasion trivial. Also, of course, I have taken advantage of colleagues and friends and of these Robert Hewison, Stefan Muthesius, Gavin Stamp and Dorothy Bosomworth were all specially helpful. Marion Johnson did the typing with a kind of professional care and caution which I always abused.

One word for Anne Williams; if we had been getting on better from 1976 to 1979 I would never have had the time to write this book. A final word for Penny Sparke, without whose more recent help and encouragement I would not have enjoyed bridging the gap between content and form quite so much . . .

Stephen Bayley
London, May 1981

'It will be the architectural work of the time
to which most attention in this country will be
called.'

Sir Charles Phipps to General Grey, 1863

Prologue

England was surprised into a very great affection for Prince Albert. It was made the more keen by the suddenness of his loss to the nation: with scarcely a presentiment of woe, Her Most Excellent Majesty's husband, Field Marshal His Royal Highness the Prince Consort, Duke of Saxony, Prince of Saxe-Coburg and Gotha, Knight of the Most Noble Order of the Garter, departed this life.[1] It was 14 December 1861, and Queen Victoria, with the nation following, had to exchange breathless, pious devotion for a life of impenetrable mourning. With her husband's death the Queen's character retired behind a veil of the thickest black crêpe, and the character of the whole country also underwent a certain change because in his twenty years as Consort to the Queen, Prince Albert, by careful husbandry of his time, had altered the face of Britain.

He had impressed by his energy and enterprise; even during student days in Bonn, in the years 1837 and 1838, a contemporary of his, Prince William of Lowenstein, had noted that Prince Albert was distinguished both by his knowledge and his diligence, by his 'quiet grace and dignity quite exceptional'.[2] On arriving in England in 1840 he soon established his authority, even over a headstrong young Queen. He instituted a working day which began at seven in the morning and continued with such vigour that both his critics and his admirers declared that his routine enabled him to pack into forty the work of eighty years.

Besides his active intervention in the political squalls of the day, Prince Albert's influence was always available in the promotion of the arts and sciences. Very early in his English career, ignoring the counsel of his advisors, he demonstrated his genuine interest in the manufacturing arts by visiting Birmingham, a city then much troubled by Chartist commotion. His biographer tells us that by the evident strength of his character Prince Albert managed to impress even the troublesome

workers. His enthusiasm for the modern world and for working-class interests went beyond cynical promotional work or condescending curiosity: he was actively involved in housing reform and presided at meetings of The Society for Improving the Conditions of the Labouring Classes. It was this same body which was responsible for building, to designs by Henry Roberts, almost the very first block of flats in Streatham Street, Bloomsbury, in 1849. In fact, it was at an official function which was an expression of his social concerns that Prince Albert first met George Gilbert Scott, the young architect, who was in future years to have his fate made historically and artistically inseparable from the Prince's. The two met in the company of Albert's uncle, Leopold, King of the Belgians, at the opening of Scott and Moffat's Infant Orphan Asylum at Wandsworth in 1843 (although nothing is recorded of any exchanges between them).[3]

The Prince's greatest contribution to national life was his proposal, made in 1849 and realized two years later, for a Great Exhibition of the Industry of all Nations, to be held in Hyde Park (Plate 1). It was an idea and a gesture as typical in its way of nineteenth-century optimism and enterprise as was Scott's memorial to its progenitor typical in equal degree of confusion in taste and superstition in matters relating to position and duty.

Towards the end of his short and active life Prince Albert began to complain more and more frequently of minor ailments, insignificant in themselves, but debilitating cumulatively. Although we know that he had a 'purity of disposition together with a cheerful, joyous spirit, and a keen sense of the ludicrous'[4] and that he often entertained his family at dinner with the gaiety of his conversation, Albert's spirit had been depleted by his public exertions and his administrative successes. At the beginning of his final illness he told the Queen, 'I do not cling to life'[5] and admitted that he would

1. Hyde Park in 1851, steel engraving from
Dafforne's *The Albert Memorial*, London, 1877.

willingly succumb to a mortal ailment which would offer him some rest from the life he was now finding so taxing. Four physicians – Sir James Clark, Sir Henry Holland, Dr Watson and Dr Jenner[6] – issued bulletins, now gloomy, now hopeful, about the prognosis of the declining Consort, but they could not pull him back from the abyss he contemplated with such equanimity. Late on that December night, when the Prince's demise seemed inevitable, the physicians sent a telegram from Windsor to the City announcing the imminent event; a little later the Prince Consort was dead and a light had gone out in England. The death of one who had – despite initial reserve about the flexibility of his Protestant persuasions – endeared himself so completely to the British people, stimulated a national movement of religious devotion to his memory, achievement and ideals. Such devotion had not always been so obvious in Prince Albert's lifetime. He was not always beloved of politicians, for instance,[7] his very real concern being occasionally mistaken for mischievousness. However, his well-founded popular reputation for probity carried him through most storms and, in any case, an unexpected death provided a splendid opportunity for ritual obsequies to be rehearsed for a palpable end and purpose.

The gloomy bureaucracy of the Victorian funeral ritual allowed the celebrants of death to indulge to the full their tastes for morbid determinism and civic occasion. On the 16th, the Monday after Prince Albert's death and the day it was announced in the daily papers, *The Times* appeared with black edgings to all its columns. Ever anxious, then as now, not to be seen to be avoiding the practical consequences of disaster, the paper assured its readers that the Queen, 'though overwhelmed with grief, bore her loss with calmness',[8] and that she would be able to continue to run the country as its sovereign even though the Consort was dead.

The funeral of Prince Albert was a solemn

toilet of the grave, giving a nation more diverse and troubled than many modern or contemporary histories allow, an opportunity to be united in the commonly appreciated pure and simple sorrow of natural mourning. Again, *The Times* noted with miserable approbation that the day of the funeral – it was 23 December 1861 – was still and gloomy. With shocking speed Victoria had had to exchange the gaiety of young marriage for the unalterable solemnity of deep and indefinite mourning – a portable tomb into which not a chink of relieving light would be allowed to penetrate. The nation sensed the Queen's grief, and Tennyson, laureate and poet to the Crown, declared in his dedication to *The Idylls of the King*, 'Break not, oh woman's heart, but still endure'.[9] The whole country followed, the Lord Mayor of London declaring on the sorrowful day of the funeral that all but the most unavoidable business should be suspended for the day. It was *The Times* that estimated the financial loss of this edict to be in the order of one million pounds.[10]

Righteous civic anxiety to memorialize the blameless Prince soon replaced the ritual exercise of national mourning. There was a widely felt popular need to pay memorial tribute to the dead Prince in a manner fitting for a nation which prided itself on its eminence in the areas of civic utility, social progress, benign legislature and international benevolence (even if it was just as popularly held that Britain could not lay claim to the same prowess in the visual arts as it could in social reforms and manufactures). The papers erupted with suggestions about a suitable Albert memorial:[11] commentators bemoaned the lack of ornament in the metropolis, comparing it unfavourably with the visual destitution of contemporary American cities. In architecture and the civic arts this was still the age of historicism, and the greater part of the popular comment about the search for an appropriate memorial was neither imaginative nor particularly adven-

turous: it rarely rose above suggestions that the
Alexandrisky column in St Petersburg be
imitated, or that the British Museum should
be encouraged to open up its convenient vaults
and offer a prototype for imitation, the Mausoleum at Halikarnassos being a suitable choice
from the Bloomsbury cornucopia and appropriate, too, in its dimensions, grandeur and
imperial associations.

At this time the memorial which was to
become forever associated with the Prince
Consort was neither proposed nor, one guesses,
even considered in its architect's mind. The
history of how the Albert Memorial which now
stands in Kensington Gardens came to be built
is a very special episode in English history and
an exquisite summary of the aspirations of
English art, frozen for us all at a peculiar
moment when national social and economic
conditions were both well disposed to encourage
architecture, sculpture and the minor arts. By
the time it was finished, Gilbert Scott had
created a fairy structure, composed half of the
builder's and half of the jeweller's art. When
it was begun Scott felt he was monumentalizing
his beloved Gothic Revival, as well as memorializing the beloved Prince. By the time he had
finished, the Albert Memorial was old-fashioned,
but Scott realized that he had created a new
style, something almost entirely original, a
style of the 1860s and of no other period, even
if its inspiration lay five centuries back. The
Albert Memorial is the work of Scott's lifetime,
as well as being in equal part a work of Prince
Albert's life too. The story of this unique
monument is the subject of this book.

1 An Idea for a Monument

Accounts of Prince Albert's funeral appeared in the daily papers of 24 December 1861. The problem facing men of affairs throughout the country was how best to utilize their regret and hand down to posterity the memory of Albert, hero of family life, institutions, colleges and workhouses. In fact, it was the Prince Consort's fate to find himself more praised and more popular in death than in life: at the end of 1861 the only memorials to his name were a few streets and public places, but once he was safely dead there was a response both instantaneous and national. Henry Cole,[1] never one to waste a moment when an opportunity for self-advancement came his way, tried to enlist support for his idea of establishing not a useless monument, but a lasting institution as a memorial to the dead Prince. Cole suggested an Albert University[2] and published his proposals in an open letter (apparently paid for by himself) which he addressed to the Earl of Granville, then Lord President of the Council, describing both the advantages and requirements of his imaginative foundation which, it was proposed, would offer degrees in both the sciences and the arts. That Cole's Albert University should be the educational equivalent of the Department of Science and Art and would, therefore, add more strength to his arm is obvious, yet in an age that prided itself on its dedication to 'usefulness', Henry Cole's admirable suggestion went entirely ignored and, it is worth noting, is still unrealized today.

With all the exquisite perception of propriety and decorum which influenced contemporary debates on meaning in the arts, *The Times* was anxious that Prince Albert, as a model of duty and affection, should inspire an appropriate memorial in public life, one whose monumentality and character would keep Great Britain ahead of her ambitious European neighbours and her rather forward offspring across the Atlantic. National concern about memorializing Prince Albert was demonstrated in *The Times*

correspondence columns. One writer, declaring to his mute audience that they should not ' . . . talk of impossibilities in these days'[3] advanced the idea that the Alexandrian monolith, given to an uncaring British people by one Mohammed Ali, who was perhaps as anxious to discharge his archaeological obligation to preserve the monument as to win favour with his distant allies, should be retrieved and brought 'home' – so that, not least, it might be saved from the 'covetous rapacity of strangers'. Although appeals for the restoration of the Alexandrian monolith, and other ancient monuments like it, were popular in the press and were often repeated subsequently by supporters urgently voicing support in a rallentando of failing conviction, the aggregate of contemporary opinion was that commentators wanted a memorial appropriate to both the age and the man.

While correspondence columns entertained earnest bores and pranksters, William Cubitt,[4] late in his career as Mayor of London and perhaps as anxious to erect a monument to his own career as much as to anything else, seized the metropolitan advantage. He published a handbill which announced a fund-raising meeting which he had organized at the Mansion House (Plate 2).

The proceedings were righteous and sombre: speakers included the Bishop of London, Lord Stratford de Redcliffe and Baron Lionel de Rothschild, who proposed the establishment of national sub-committees to gather funds for a future memorial. A report of Cubitt's meeting, its text running to fifty-eight column inches, punctuated here and there by parenthetical cheers indicative of the animation which charged the meeting, soon appeared in *The Times*.[5] All those present were concerned with public life and determined that some sort of lasting memorial should be created. Cubitt defined the basis of the meeting: those present, he said, 'deeply deplored the irreparable loss

CUBITT, MAYOR.

A PUBLIC MEETING

will be held on TUESDAY NEXT, in the *Egyptian Hall*, at the *Mansion House*, to consider the propriety of inviting Contributions, for the purpose of erecting a lasting Memorial to His late Royal Highness the PRINCE CONSORT, and to adopt such measures for carrying out the object, as may then be decided on.

The Right Hon. the LORD MAYOR will take the Chair at TWO o'clock precisely.

MANSION HOUSE,
9th January, 1862.

the country has sustained by the lamented death of His Royal Highness The Prince Consort, whose powerful and well-regulated mind, and great abilities, have . . . been unceasingly devoted to improving the conditions of the humbler classes, and to the development and extension of Science and Art . . . '[6] The whole meeting concurred in the idea that a lasting and tangible memorial, expressive of popular gratitude for a life devoted to public benefit, should be erected for Prince Albert. It was also declared that whatever form the proposed memorial should take, it should in any case be 'monumental and national in character'[7] and that it should be approved by the Queen. It was this last point which was crucial in the history of 'the' Albert Memorial.

Cubitt's meeting was characterized throughout by a Revivalist energy and enthusiasm: one MP present, a certain H. Lewis, expressed a popular idea when in the course of the discussion he declared that 'we should never lose sight of the fact that the Prince Consort had a very deep sense of religion, which pervaded his whole mind.'[8] What this means, in mid-nineteenth-century terms, is that such a 'deep sense of religion' virtually excluded a 'pagan', that is to say classical, monument. This, together with the introduction of the Queen, not known for her enthusiasm for Greek or Roman architecture, into the judging procedure, effectively secured the Albert Memorial as a gain for the Goths. Furthermore, it was at this meeting in the Mansion House that a Committee was appointed to obtain public funds for the erection of a memorial appropriate to the dimensions of a nation's regard, and it is here that the history of George Gilbert Scott's Albert Memorial, the one in Kensington Gardens, begins.

Any contemporary chronicler would have marvelled at the manner in which a major public monument was to be created out of spontaneously generated popular concern. At this stage there was no 'official' interference, nor any 'official' support besides, yet it was some time before Scott's Albert Memorial was designed, not to speak of the time which was to elapse before it was begun or completed.[9] What repertoire of ideas about the character and the appearance of monuments did the age have to offer?

From the historical past, a few examples proposed themselves as prototypes which were consonant with the taste of the 1860s: perhaps Balducci's shrine of St Peter Martyr at San Eustorgio, Milan, erected in 1339, and Peter Vischer's shrine of St Sebaldus at Nuremberg of 1506–12; besides these, Henry Cole's museum contained a handful of models suitable for emulation, but as for contemporary monuments which might provide inspiration, Europe was rather better equipped then than was England: from the recent past there was little to speak of by way of monuments in England, save the Nelson Column in Trafalgar Square and the George III memorial at Weymouth.

The modern revival of an open shrine, which was to become Scott's idea for the Albert Memorial, appears to have had its origins in Germany, where Karl Friedrich Schinkel's designs of stage sets for Hoffmann and Fouqué's opera, *Undine*, of 1816 provide a theatrical precedent for a fantastic Gothic structure which, although it contains no statue, is immediately reminiscent of Scott's secular shrine in Kensington (Plate 3).[10] Schinkel also made monuments in the classical manner, most especially the tomb of Louisa of Mecklenberg-Strelitz, Queen of Prussia, built in a pure Greek Revival style in the Charlottenburg by Gentz after a design by Schinkel,[11] but it was another German monument which was to provide the most often remarked upon prototype for admiration by English observers. This was Christian Daniel Rauch's bronze monument to Frederick the Great (Plate 4); such was the

3. Karl Friedrich Schinkel, 'Platz in der Reichstadt', 1816. Gouache drawing for a scene from Hoffmann and Fouqué's *Undine* (*Kupferstichkabinett, Staatliche Museen zu Berlin-Ost*).

4. Christian Daniel Rauch, monument to Frederick the Great, Berlin (*Courtauld Institute of Art*).

5. George Meickle Kemp, Walter Scott Memorial,
Edinburgh, 1836 (*National Monuments Record*).

celebrity of this monument that in a competition entry for the Kensington Albert Memorial, Sir James Pennethorne, quoting from the initial instructions to architects, referred to Rauch's statue as 'among the finest monuments of modern times',[12] and Sir Charles Eastlake, while Chairman of the Albert Memorial Committee during 1863, wrote to Gustav Waagen, head of the Berlin Museum, to ask whether in his experience the bronze which Rauch had so successfully used in Berlin would tolerate the more corrosive London climate.[13]

Despite the snooty condescension of *The Times*, which considered Britain backward in the field of civic monuments,[14] it was the British Isles which furnished one of the most substantial and notorious of all nineteenth-century monuments and one which Gilbert Scott must certainly have known. That no author or correspondent in *The Times* referred to it can merely be taken as an indication that George Meickle Kemp's Walter Scott Memorial in Edinburgh (Plate 5) was temporarily not in favour.[15] Ruskin gives us an idea of its status: in a peculiarly acid passage from *Fors Clavigera* he calls it a small, vulgar, Gothic steeple',[16] a comment which suggests as much as anything else that Ruskin may not always have been as observant as his reputation suggests: while Kemp's Scott Memorial may be considered as 'vulgar' as you like, whatever else might be the case, it is certainly not small: it is almost 200 feet tall.

The lives of Kemp and Scott were incongruous, although Kemp had, in fact, met Scott while on one of his walking trips between Peebles and Galashiels. The more famous English architect gave Kemp a lift, but he did not at the time know the identity of his benefactor. Even if their careers, social backgrounds and professional futures could hardly have been more divergent, the circumstances which attended the creation of Kemp's Scott Memorial and Gilbert Scott's Albert Memorial were similar in character. It is interesting to note that Scott never refers to Kemp's earlier Memorial in any of his preserved writings.

Public meetings in Scotland suggested that the rhapsodist of Highland lore be afforded a striking memorial on his death, an architectural complement to the prodigious literary memorial which he had already left behind. What happened with the Scott Memorial demonstrates much of the concern which public bodies felt about the propriety of memorials in the nineteenth century: the preliminary meeting, held on 11 December 1835, passed a resolution that 'no architectural monument should be adopted of which a statue cannot form a part',[17] a portrait statue being in this case the only feature which, it was felt, could adequately guarantee popular recognition of the purpose of the memorial. Then again, in a pattern which was to become familiar throughout the century, the organizing committee invited designs for a monument which would combine statuary and architecture in a suitably emblematic manner. The upper limit of cost was set at £5,000, and fifty-four designs were received: twenty-two were Gothic, eleven were simple statues, fourteen were Greek Revival temples, five were monumental columns and there was one fountain and one obelisk. From this original competition it was Thomas Rickman, architect and historian of Gothic architecture, who won the first premium of fifty guineas; a London sculptor called R. W. Siever came second and George Meickle Kemp was placed only third. Kemp, who had previously engaged himself on some abortive projects like an album of drawings of Scottish ecclesiastical remains, based his design on Melrose Abbey. It took him a bare five days to complete.

The Scottish committee was not satisfied with the result of the original competition and it now invited David Roberts, RA, to submit a design. When this was also rejected, the Committee reconsidered the merits of Kemp's design, and although at first it was placed only third, it was generally accepted as adequate, with only a few committee members cavilling at the architect's lack of status: he was virtually unknown, but achieved some celebrity when he drowned in the Union Canal in 1844.

At about the same time that Kemp's Scott Memorial was being built in Edinburgh there was also a single famous example in France of an emblematic memorial which united sculpture and architecture into a monumental whole. This was Charles-Auguste Questel's design for a monumental fountain, enriched with sculpture by Jean-Jacques Pradier, built on the Esplanade at Nîmes in 1848.[18] This monumental fountain which at least caught the attention of Sir Charles Eastlake, was at the centre of a basin whose circumference measured forty metres; Pradier's sculptures ornamented the whole, those at the corners depicting 'le Rhône', 'le Gardon', 'la Fontaine de Nîmes' and 'la Fontaine d'Eure', and a figure representing the city of Nîmes stood at the summit of the ensemble.[19]

Meanwhile, in England, the young and energetic Gilbert Scott (Plate 6) had been under the influence of Pugin, as, indeed, most young architects were at that time.[20] Particularly in the period when Scott's own work began to move away from the utilitarian essays of his early career towards a realization of the full possibilities of the Gothic Revival, the example of the messianic Pugin must have seemed specially strong. This was the period when Scott designed his first essay in monumental architecture, the Martyrs' Memorial in Oxford (Plate 7), and he found himself, while still relatively little known, a celebrated figure. For his design Scott fell back on studies he had made ten years before, in 1840, of the surviving Eleanor Crosses – those at Geddington, Northampton and Waltham – which Edward I had erected at various points where Queen Eleanor's body had rested on its final journey to London from Nottinghamshire. In his preparation for the Martyrs' Memorial Scott, in typically thorough fashion, obtained every drawing he could of old crosses and, even though his design was made during the period before his awakening to a 'true feeling for church [i.e. Gothic] architecture', he confidently felt that his first monumental design was 'better than anyone but Pugin could then have provided'.[21] Although a fine monument of its kind, the Martyrs' Memorial is typical of the first phase of the nineteenth-century Gothic Revival: compared to the Kensington Memorial with its richness and visual complexity, it appears thin and brittle, almost like a Commissioners' church beside an Ecclesiologist's cathedral.

There was a handful of other contemporary attempts to define the form of an appropriate nineteenth-century memorial to a distinguished figure. The sculptor, Thomas Woolner, before his departure for Australia (an event itself memorialized in Ford Madox Brown's painting, *The Last of England*) submitted a design with 'symbolical figures' for a proposed Wordsworth Memorial during May 1851.[22] At about the same time, Pietro Tenerani's monument to Pope Pius VIII, built in St Peter's between 1853 and 1866, also enjoyed some popular acclaim as a prototype for a modern monument which combined architecture with sculpture in an illustrative and didactic way.[23]

Even before the rash of Albert Memorials had erupted over Britain on Albert's death, there were many provincial, vernacular prototypes for Scott's ultimately successful design. These were the drinking fountains which were once so common a feature in British towns. Typical of the genre was the one which Alex Randall left to his native Maidstone, erected in the Market Place in 1862: here, an emblematic figure stands upon a plinth, covered by an open Gothic shrine with a spire, with sculpted figures on top of the angle capitals.

These various faltering attempts to find a suitable architectural expression for a modern

6. George Richmond, RA, portrait of George Gilbert Scott (*Royal Academy of Arts*).

7. George Gilbert Scott, the Martyrs' Memorial, Oxford, 1841–3 (*National Monuments Record*).

monument were all synthesized in the national rush of woe which followed Prince Albert's death. Authorities and architects, activists and commentators searched Europe and home for models fitted to their interpretation of the Prince Consort's prestige, for such was the mood of the time that truly original architectural ideas were scarcely imaginable, let alone realizable.

Funereal righteousness promoted a galaxy of memorializing activity: in February 1862, Liverpool Town Council voted £5,000 for an equestrian statue by Thornycroft to be erected by the east front of Harvey Lonsdale Elmes' St George's Hall.[24] It was finished five years later. Also in February, 1862, Glasgow proposed a memorial to be executed by Marochetti,[25] and by 1864 Albert's death had occasioned in Wales 'the enrolment of a large part of the higher classes'[26] – 16,500 of them, in fact – in fund-raising activities which culminated in the erecting in Tenby of an Albert Memorial with a statue by John Evan Thomas and a plinth by H Maule Finch.[27] In Cambridge a Committee was convened to discuss the most fitting material and site for an Albert Memorial,[28] and in Halifax, Thornycroft, again, was to erect a statue.[29] A public meeting was held in Alderney during December 1862 to discuss plans for a memorial; a year later plans were being made in Aberdeen.[30] The authorities in Weston-super-Mare got close to the spirit which animated Prince Albert when they dedicated their Albert Memorial Industrial Night School to the memory of the Prince in 1863 (Plate 8);[31] William Brodie sculpted an Albert in the robes of the Order of the Thistle for Perth, and a Matthew Noble was commissioned by the Bath Albert Memorial Committee to execute a colossal bust for a new building to be added to Bath United Hospital; Bradford proposed an Albert Institution along the lines of an Association for Education of Designers and Skilled Workmen; an Albert Memorial Bridge was proposed in Victoria Park, and at Gravesend St Thomas'

Almshouses was endowed in the Prince's memory.[32] A window of Christ Church, Banbury, was dedicated to Prince Albert, a project for a statue was begun in Abingdon and, finally in a list exhaustive in its geographical and imaginative extent, a School of Art was proposed in Devon.[33]

It was Manchester, however, which before London made the biggest municipal gesture towards Prince Albert's memory. In the year after the Prince's death, Thomas Worthington's design for a Manchester Albert Memorial appeared.[34] The published design in *The Builder*, showing an elaborate Gothic shrine covering a statue, standing on a plinth bearing the inscription 'Albert the Great and the Good', shows how firmly associated in architects' minds the Gothic cross formula had become (even before Gilbert Scott's synoptic design): in every respect, from architectural form through to civic responsibility, Worthington's design was a precedent to Scott's (Plate 9).

There had been a wide response in Manchester to a local committee's idea of commemorating Prince Albert: popular financial support came from the No. 1 Hydraulic Packers Society (who offered 13s 10d) and Manchester Corporation (which offered £500).[35] Proposals were received for a drinking fountain, six model cottages, a museum of arts and sciences, a park (for the deprived area of Hulme), a tower for the cathedral, an 'In Memoriam Fund' for the Infirmary, public baths, a Walhalla, an orphanage, a school of science, the conversion of the Botanical Gardens into a public park, a convalescent hospital and a lending library.[36] However, the funds available were more limited than the variety of proposals, and because the Mayor had already undertaken to provide a statue (to be executed by Noble), the type of monument which could be erected was limited to something along the lines of Kemp's Scott Memorial in Edinburgh.[37] The design chosen was that sub-

May it please Your Majesty,

We the undersigned, Your Majesty's loyal and dutiful subjects, crave permission to submit to Your Majesty the following details in connexion with the erection of the Albert Memorial Industrial Night School Buildings at Weston Super Mare.

8. Drawing for the Albert Memorial Industrial Night School, Weston-super-Mare, 1863 (*HM The Queen*).

9. Thomas Worthington, the Albert Memorial, Manchester, 1862–7 (*National Monuments Record*).

mitted by Thomas Worthington. He chose a medieval-style canopy of white stone, open on four sides, with each opening spanned by pointed arches, surmounted by gablets. Although its dimensions were modest,[38] this effect was offset by the 'rich and elaborate' design which Worthington imagined was Tuscan, somewhere between the styles of Giotto and Brunelleschi. Above each gablet there were angels blowing trumpets, and in the contemporary description, considerable emphasis was given to the richness and elaboration of the carving, which was remarkable indeed by comparison with the austere Infirmary in front of which Worthington's Memorial was intended to stand. The visual complexity and interest of an imitation

fourteenth-century style was by no means a universally accepted taste in 1862: when the design for Worthington's Manchester Albert Memorial appeared in that year it was, perhaps, ahead of popular taste.

Scott has nothing to say about Worthington's design; he may have repressed all memories of it, but he must certainly have known it. However, whether it was a precedent or not, Scott's memorial in Kensington is a much greater artistic achievement: in the dimensions of the imagination employed and in the combination of architecture with sculpture and the applied arts, Scott found an architectural equivalent of that combination of domestic and public virtue which marked Prince Albert's life.

2 The Competition for the Albert Memorial

Henry Cole's useful proposal that there might be an Albert University, offering technical and vocational degrees in both the arts and the sciences to the greater glory of the memory of the departed Prince Consort, was made at the end of 1861, only two weeks after Prince Albert's death and even before the metropolitan worthies had assembled themselves under Cubitt's tutelage to discuss a formal memorial at the Mansion House.[1] There can be little doubt that this idea of Cole's had been prepared for some time, filed near the top drawer of his desk against the possibility of a suitably heroic demise, and was published privately only when the pretext of Prince Albert's death provided splendid protective cover for Cole's monomaniac enterprise; but Cole himself was aware that however forcefully he might argue the case for an institutional memorial in the form of an industrial university, this monument, no matter how rational or relevant to Prince Albert's expressed wishes, would not satisfy the public's appetite for a more emotional and more artistic memorial.[2] By the end of the first week in January 1862, Cole had remanoeuvred himself and was busy supplementing his University proposal with the idea that, out of a notional parliamentary grant of £100,000, £20,000 should be spent on an obelisk to supplement by art the functional memorial of an Albert University which Cole had proposed.[3]

Although Cole could scarcely have realized it, his own taste for an obelisk was exactly congruent with the Queen's idea of what a memorial should be: the Committee which had found itself elected at the Mansion House meeting, now found itself at a second meeting, a month after the first, rather at a loss about how best to proceed because it was then ignorant of the Queen's wishes and preferences. Cubitt wrote to General Grey,[4] then acting as the Queen's private secretary, delicately soliciting Her Majesty's opinions and tastes on the matter. The Queen, who declared herself on more than one occasion to have no taste in matters of art[5] (relying in this, as in other respects, on Albert in life, as in death), fell back on the familiar and easy idea of having an obelisk on the site of the Great Exhibition. Her Majesty was, however, anxious 'provided it is in a style of sufficient grandeur'[6] to match her own and her public's estimation of Albert's worth. Grey went further in suggesting how deeply implanted in the royal mind was the notion of an elaborate and richly decorated Albert Memorial when he transmitted to the Committee an idea, no doubt the Queen's, that 'several of the first artists of the day might take part in its execution, for there would be room at the base of the obelisk for various groups of statuary, each of which might be entrusted to a different artist.'[7]

Sir Charles Eastlake,[8] who had known Albert from the Royal Fine Art Commission, was chosen as the Queen's personal artistic adviser after Henry Cole had taken advice from the painter, Mulready: Eastlake was described as 'patriarch of the Royal Academy and the most cautious and prudent of men',[9] qualities which would have recommended him to this royal appointment; later, he was to become the unquestioned authority on the Gothic Revival. Eastlake was backed up by a Committee on which he sat himself, together with the Earls of Derby and Clarendon, and Cubitt, whose general brief it was to advise the Queen on the choice of design, the execution of the Memorial and the selection of artists.[10] The Committee met first at the Earl of Derby's house in St James's Square, and regarded it as its duty to consider the various unsolicited proposals – not least those from the Queen – which were a testimony to the fact that public and personal interest in the Memorial was being kept alive by occasional and spirited reports in *The Times*.

The idea of an obelisk, then enjoying some temporary celebrity, was one which was very dear to Her Majesty[11] and a cause for lively debate among those interested in the arts:

Joseph Bonomi had advised Eastlake on the architectural sources and character of obelisks,[12] and William Tite told him that the Royal Institute of British Architects had even formed a committee to consider them;[13] John Gibson, then styling himself 'scultore inglesi a Roma', and doubtless anxious for a commission, attacked the obelisk idea on grounds of historical inconsistency, and proposed instead a Mausoleum, a type of monument he considered a more profitable vehicle for the demonstration of his talents.[14] The sculptor Gibson's objections do, of course, have their point, as the derivative idea of an obelisk merely afforded an opportunity for the civic authorities to indulge their taste for attempting to equal or even to outstrip the ancients; Eastlake recorded in a note to General Grey during March 1862 that ' . . . some of the committee think it desirable to surpass, if possible, the highest existing *ancient* example',[15] adding, almost parenthetically, that the Lateran obelisk, a model for imitation, was not quite 106 feet tall.

In thinking about the possibilities of erecting a purpose-built, as opposed to borrowed or found, obelisk to Prince Albert's memory, the Committee had first to consider what material to use; if stone, was the structure to be a monolith or composed of separate drums, and would 'Russian Finland' (the Queen's suggestion) or Scotland furnish the best granite for the obelisk of eighty to a hundred feet that was being officially considered?[16] (An engineer wrote in, while the Committee was pondering these matters, suggesting the use of iron which would allow a height of 500 feet – unrivalled by either ancients or moderns – to be attained.[17]) However, the Committee experienced considerable difficulty in locating a stretch of granite of sufficient proportions to make an impressive monolithic obelisk. When the right colour was found, its consistency was too soft, or the vein was too small. The Duke of Argyll, owner of the Ross of Mull quarries, was alerted by some

means to the problem, and stepped in with a claim to have excavated a portion of granite whose length was already 114 feet, but there were doubts about whether the narrowness in its middle reaches would sustain in a free standing state, the thrust of the upper parts which its length would impose.[18]

Throughout March and April 1862, the period running up to the submission of the Committee's original Report, Eastlake and the others had also to consider various unsolicited and cranky proposals for a monument, many of them very alarming and all of them characteristic in equal part of contemporary enthusiasm, optimism and architectural naïveté. One Delabere Barker suggested that the proposed Memorial's 'dimensions should as far exceed all existing Monuments of departed worth, as the Prince's virtues so far exceeded all others'.[19] To this end, Barker proposed an obelisk some 550 feet tall, made out of two-tone granite, decorated around the base with statuary providing an emblematic epitome of Prince Albert's illustrious life. Prophetically, Barker also proposed that at each corner of the base there should be a sculptural group showing the four continents in appropriate attitudes of mourning, together with some more sculpture 'emblematic of the grand divisions of human industry' which were, in his plan, to be on the higher portions of the base.[20] The Rev. J. A. E. Merton, to mention only one other enthusiast, petitioned first the Earl of Granville, Lord President of the Council, and then Eastlake, with his idea of a 'Temple of Peace' as the most fitting Albert Memorial.[21]

The famous also joined in to tax Eastlake's patience: F. T. Palgrave, anthologist, *inter alia*, of *The Golden Treasury*, regretted the lack of adventure so far shown and tried to whip up support for the deflating idea of a monolithic obelisk; he even published an article about it, allowing only that if a *building* were to be the chosen memorial, then it should not be Byzantine, even though he maintained that this was

Albert's preferred style, because, given the age's preferences in art, it would, he felt, be too hazardous an experiment in taste.[22]

The painter William Dyce wrote a letter in rhapsodic style to Eastlake, proposing the tomb of the Emperor Maximilian at Innsbruck as a suitable prototype for a British memorial.[23] This notion gave Dyce a fine opportunity to make heavy weather of the biblical references upon which the Innsbruck tomb relied for its effect and which were, simultaneously, becoming dominant themes in his own paintings: Dyce said the Maximilian tomb was based on a passage from Isaiah, in fact, 14:9, which represents the commotion and stirring-up of the departments of Hades on the descent of a great and heroic spirit after a lifetime of toil. Dyce thought this biblical theme would furthermore provide an opportunity for combining groups and single figures in statuary, his notion of the monument being that 'there should be a sort of mortuary chapel or Temple in the centre of which stands – a tomb on which the Hero-prince should be represented in an attitude of repose and around this statues and groups of heroic men and women of all times'.[24] The idea of a Parnassus, which was so to distinguish Gilbert Scott's successful design, was already firmly established in the minds of men concerned with art.

Of architects, both Jakob Ignaz Hittorff and Alexander Thomson were men with a European reputation who appear to have prepared unsolicited designs: Hittorff's sketches (Plate 10) were made in 1862 and dedicated to Thomas Donaldson, whom he described as his 'ancien et dévoué ami'.[25] Donaldson, who was the author of Hittorff's obituary notice in the Royal Institute of British Architects *Transactions* (and whose opinion of Scott might be estimated from knowing that he had attempted to have reversed the Royal Institute's proposed award of a Royal Medal to him),[26] must have told his friend Hittorff about all the activity in

London, and the idea of providing a design for an Albert Memorial (an architectural genre he had never before attempted) must have appealed to his imagination: he produced designs in a cinquecento style, not unlike his Gare du Nord in Paris, which was apsidal with an open front and fountains on three sides: the apse surrounded a statue that did not, from Hittorff's drawings, look one bit like the Prince. 'Greek' Thomson's design, on the other hand, was monumental and in his own idiosyncratic version of the Greek Revival (Plate 11).[27] James Fergusson, the historian, author of *A History of Architecture in All Countries*, also seems to have attempted a design.[28]

This international interest in providing a design for a future Albert Memorial was all *ex camera* of the Committee Room where the real decisions about the future and the form of the Albert Memorial were being made. On 14 April 1862, the Committee had submitted its first *Report* to the Queen which effectively saw the end of providing an obelisk, saying after a provision that if it was built it would look incomplete, 'nor can we refrain from expressing our serious doubts whether even if the mere enterprise were successful, the ultimate effect would be such as to realize your Majesty's just and natural expectations'.[29] The Queen, plainly, was intended to descend, as it were, from the obelisk and in this action she eventually acquiesced. Grey was her agent to Eastlake, and wrote on 19 April 1862 that it was Queen Victoria's wish that the committee should 'turn their attention to the possibility of finding some other mode in which the great object in view may be most satisfactorily effected'.[30] As we have seen, the Queen was always rather at a loss in matters of art, relying in his lifetime and afterwards as well on her husband's taste, and she now left the Committee free, only suggesting that 'the foremost architects of the day' might be invited to submit proposals for combining statuary with architecture.[31] The obelisk idea,

10. Jakob Ignaz Hittorff, proposal for an Albert Memorial (*Wallraf-Richartz Museum, Cologne*).

11. Alexander 'Greek' Thomson, proposal for an Albert Memorial (*Architectural Review. Photo: Royal Institute of British Architects*).

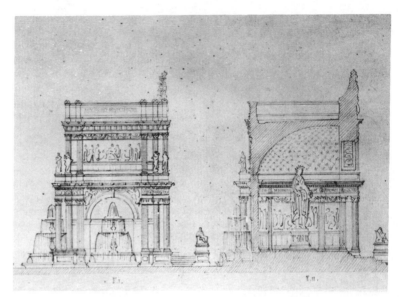

once official, was now officially dead: it was the announcement of this to the general public, in *The Times* of 22 April 1862, that may have stimulated the various speculative responses, although Hittorff was probably tipped off by his friend Donaldson.

What was the Committee to do, faced with a restive populace, an inconsolable Queen anxious for a memorial to a beloved husband, and an international interest in the outcome of their deliberations? The Committee's *Minutes* for 30 April 1862 record that Eastlake had gone to see the architects, Tite and Smirke, presumably to seek their advice on the Queen's new proposal.[32] Within two weeks the Committee had resolved to invite some prominent architects to a meeting at the Royal Fine Art Commission to be held on 16 May 1862; they were George Gilbert Scott, William Tite, Philip Hardwick, James Pennethorne, Sidney Smirke, Thomas Donaldson and Matthew Digby Wyatt.[33] Scott was the only Goth chosen to consult with the six leading classical architects of the day, and he was not a little wary of being included with some individuals who, as he told Eastlake in a letter declining to come to the first meeting on account of being promised forth in Paris, 'have taken an active part in defeating my wishes as to the style of the only public building in which I have been engaged in London', [34] an all-too-clear reference to the Foreign Office *débâcle* in which Scott was forced by Palmerston into making artistic compromises which tested his nerve as much as his taste (see Chapter 3, note 40).

Scott had no wish to be a part of any heterogeneous group offering advice; he wanted to act alone, rightly thinking that the grandees of classicism would overwhelm a sole Goth. His own idea about a memorial was that it should 'go rather in the direction of a medieval cross as the centre of the group',[35] but he did not see much chance of getting this idea across to the likes of Smirke and Hardwick. With a dedication

to solitary action which was remarkable, Scott wanted the chance to furnish his own design, not to take part in a collective effort: 'their united opinion', he said in a private note to Eastlake, 'would be a *caput mortuum*'.[36]

At the Royal Fine Arts Commission meeting held while Scott was in Paris, Eastlake told the assembled architects of General Grey's proposal of a 'combination, if possible, of a monument with an institution for education in Science and Art as applied to productive industry'.[37] The idea of a single, monumental memorial was not yet clear in anyone's mind. Eastlake's correspondence indicates that he was turning over many ideas himself, even as he was inviting other opinions from the seven chosen architects. He admired, for instance, Pradier and Questel's fountain at Nimes[38] and wanted to take this as an example of how architecture and sculpture might most effectively be united in a single monument. More and more the idea was forming in Eastlake's mind that a memorial – 'a monument in the plain meaning of the word,' he wrote to Grey[39] – should be the primary aim of the Prince Consort Memorial Committee and that, if necessary, any other intrusive ideas should take second place to it.

Egregious amongst all the second-runners in the competition for the Committee's attention was, of course, Henry Cole's proposal for an industrial university, which with increasing realism was by now slowly beginning to develop into the more modest idea of an Albert Hall, a project which was later to become popularly known as the 'Cole Hole'. It was Eastlake's thankless task to deal with men as difficult as Henry Cole. In emphasizing at official level the outstanding claims of a monument pure and simple, Eastlake might be regarded as slighting Cole, at least in the view of Cole himself, who was always quick to see predatory gestures. Eastlake wrote: 'The project of the hall will I hope be entertained but on consideration I think it will be necessary to adhere to the

monument, as such, and to place it in Hyde
Park . . . It is possible that the scheme for the
hall may, for want of funds, lead only to a
recommendation that it should be erected for a
central place of meeting . . . '[40] Cole, never a
man to be caught short when seeking a reference,
personal or historical, to support any campaign
he was momentarily backing, fell on the idea
that many 'societies' – he was probably thinking
of the Royal Society of Arts – would find an
Albert Hall useful, but this was not enough to
save the idea, at least for the moment.

With the architects, Tite was Eastlake's
go-between, and he wrote on 20 June 1862,
giving an assurance that the chosen architects,
'with few exceptions' (who, in fact, turned out
to be Tite and Smirke), would be ready to
'furnish designs for the general character of the
Memorial'.[41] Plans of the site, confirmed by
Eastlake, following Her Majesty's wishes, as
that patch of land just north of the then
Kensington Road, now Kensington Gore (the
space south, between Kensington Road and the
Horticultural Conservatory, being reserved for
the putative Hall), were lithographed and
eventually sent out to architects, together with
an instructive letter whose contents were considered at a meeting held during July 1862.[42]

What did the Queen want of the Memorial?
She considered it indispensable that the monument should contain, at least, a portrait statue
of Albert, and that it should stand in the open
air.[43] This was in accordance with the initial
Report which, besides recommending the now
disposed obelisk idea, suggested as well a
column, a Gothic cross, a large group of sculpture and, with irritating allusiveness, 'a
building': all these solutions were amenable to
Queen Victoria's wishes.

Eastlake, however, before he even knew what
the architects who had been invited to send in
designs might produce, had diplomatically to
advise Grey to encourage the Queen to loosen
her inflexible grip on the matter of the design:

'An open monument with bronze statues may be
the ultimate result but it is quite possible that
something strikingly new and good of another
kind may be thought of'.[44]

The letter to architects was sent out on 19
July 1862, fifteen days after the meeting had
been held to consider its contents. In it the
seven chosen architects were invited to submit
designs for a memorial to Prince Albert, and
they were sent to help them in their task plans
of the site, the second *Report of the Prince
Consort Memorial Committee*, a copy of Grey's
letter in reply to it, the first architects' *Report*
and copies of the correspondence between the
Prince Consort Memorial Committee and the
Commissioners for the Exhibition of 1851.[45] The
letter, rather peremptorily, required architects
to give their assent or signal their dissent
promptly as well as asking that they discuss the
matter with no one: the official papers had not
yet gone before Parliament, and it was felt that
premature publication might prejudice the
successful outcome of the grand project which
was everyone's shared concern.

Donaldson replied on 23 July 1862,[46] Scott's
reply, a scrupulously careful letter, checking
whether funding was adequate for the proposals
intended, was acknowledged on the same day as
Donaldson's;[47] Pennethorne was anxious as to
whether architecture was going to be subservient
to sculpture in the Memorial,[48] and by way of
reply Eastlake referred him to Pradier and
Questel's fountain;[49] Charles Barry wanted his
design entered jointly under his name and that
of his partner, Banks, while he also wanted
other architects invited as well, a suggestion
which Eastlake rejected;[50] Hardwick accepted;[51]
Tite and Smirke both declined, Smirke on
account of his age (he was eighty-one), saying
that the competition was for younger architects.[52] Edward Barry filled the gap left by Tite
and Smirke.

The designs received from this canvass were
to be displayed to the Queen in her fastness at

12. P. C. Hardwick, competition design: detail
showing statue of Prince Albert (*Royal Institute
of British Architects*).

Windsor; they were to be in by 1 December,[53]
and great secrecy – for a militant Press was
hinted at – was to attend their display:
Eastlake wrote to Pennethorne, at the time of
the exhibition of the designs to Her Majesty,
saying that the glass in one of his frames had
been inadvertently smashed, but that in the
course of replacement only workmen would
see it.[54] On this occasion, all the drawings were
to be covered by a cloth until the Queen arrived
on judging day.

These are the designs she saw, shown to her
by the nation's best architects fourteen months
after Prince Albert's death.

P. C. Hardwick's design

P. C. Hardwick, who took over his father's
practice in 1861,[55] did not, at least according to
The Builder, over-extend himself in his efforts:
that paper said 'Mr Hardwick contents himself
with a design for a group of sculpture and
Pedestal',[56] a rather mealy-mouthed description
of what, in fact, was a design which was very
much more elaborate than that (Plates 12–14).
In some additional, explanatory notes, the
younger Hardwick explained his artistic intentions to Eastlake:

In the monument itself I have endeavoured to
point to the illustrious career of the Prince
Consort in promoting the *Arts of Peace*, and the
benefits which he thus conferred on the world. I
have therefore placed at his feet a figure
representing Peace, who is holding up to him a
wreath of oak. On either side are figures
representing *Art* and *Science*, in the promotion of
which His Royal Highness had devoted so large a
portion of his life. At the back of the copper
pedestal is a trophy with the shields of England and
Saxe-Coburg Gotha; upon the lowest pedestal will
be found to be that which, while it makes the most
prominent and important object in the monument,
will prevent it from being disproportionate to the
rest of the composition.[57]

13. P. C. Hardwick, competition design for the Albert Memorial, 1862: general view (*Royal Institute of British Architects*).

14. P. C. Hardwick, competition design: distant view (*Royal Institute of British Architects*).

The statue on Hardwick's memorial design was to be of gilded bronze and the pedestal of polished granite, and the architect estimated the cost at £48,000.[58] What Hardwick modestly forebore to explain was the fantastic architectural programme he conceived for what is teasingly called in his description a 'pedestal' for the heroic, gilt Prince: a lower range of steps flanked by piers, each carrying reminiscences of the original obelisk idea, lead to a pool, flanked by potted trees, whose central feature is an elaborate piece of emblematic statuary where water spews from an allegorical figure placed in a conch, surrounded by indeterminate mythological beasts. At the rear of this pool two ranges of balustraded steps give on to a plateau from which the steps to the climactic pedestal are gained. The pedestal is the central, culminating feature of Hardwick's design: it is of semicircular construction where the two open ends are niches topped by pediments with sculpture. Profuse flora, urns and gaslights add an air of business and variety to the memorial structure, whose central artistic purpose was to provide a means of viewing Albert's statue, surrounded by minor didactic and historical statuary intended to demonstrate the fruitful commerce between Prince Albert and the Arts and Sciences. To add verisimilitude, Hardwick's competition drawings show members of the public graciously disporting themselves around the lower reaches of the pedestal.

T. L. Donaldson's design

Professor Donaldson submitted fourteen drawings of a design for a hemicycle enriched with emblematic statuary and mural painting, which featured a gigantic statue of Albert some thirty feet high (Plate 15).[59] He said of this 'important subject':

It has been my endeavour to avoid the imitation of any existing monument of this class, and to create one which should be original in its conception and treatment; thus preventing any

parallel being instituted between it and any other.[60]

The idea of the open shrine was not only to leave the statue permanently visible, but also to forestall the corrosive depredations which the London atmosphere might make on Prince Albert's image. The architect fondly hoped that it might equally recall the effect of the chryselephantine figure of Athena which Phidias had made for the Parthenon.

Inside the open shrine there was a den of inventive and allusive genius, with Donaldson's suggestions of how the first artists of the day might represent, in both direct and associative ways, the 'associations of his [Prince Albert's] own high taste and learning'.[61] Lighting was to come only from the open sides, so that no disrespectful top-light should disfigure the representation of the noble Prince.

It was Donaldson's intention that his Albert Memorial should reflect 'the refined, the tranquil, the unpretending spirit of the Prince. The sufferings of a martyr are lost in the glory of his translation', he avers, and 'The character of the shrine should have nothing of a sombre aspect; it should not bear the appearance of a temple nor of a tomb, for the Prince's remains lie elsewhere.'[62] The better to achieve this effect of memorial levity which he desired, Donaldson designed in the Corinthian order – which he felt to be 'cheerful' – and fountains played around, to express the animation which charged the Prince's mind. To allay any premature fears about the grotesque possibility of a statuesque Prince Albert streaming with damp, Donaldson made the thoughtful provision of a hypocaust in the basement to keep the cheerful, animated air dry. He also felt, in view of the weather, that it might be expedient to glaze the open sides of the shrine.[63]

Donaldson included in his submission a design for the Albert Hall, proposed for the adjacent site, whose main feature would, again, be a monumental statue of the Prince flanked by

15. T. L. Donaldson, competition design for the
Albert Memorial, 1862 (*Royal Institute of British
Architects*).

'emblematical figures' and a mural painting, running in a band eight feet high, illustrating the history of the arts, sciences and literature, with enamel heads of illustrious personages above, around three sides of the building. Donaldson compared his concept to Flandrin's saints in the church of St Vincent de Paul, Paris, but all his own was the idea of including speculative housing on the adjoining land so that the lure of his masterpiece might also gain the 'most productive rental'[64] in this development area. Donaldson's total estimate, including engines for the waterworks, was set at £70,000.

Sir James Pennethorne's design
Sir James Pennethorne completed, and printed, his design in December 1862. He submitted nine drawings for a memorial whose total cost he estimated would be £68,850.[65]

Pennethorne thought that there was no point in an obelisk, unless it could be a monolith (and that idea had, in any case, by now been discredited); the column and the Gothic cross were, he said, discounted because they might make the statue on which the Queen insisted look too small; sculpture, he went on, would have to be of bronze to withstand the assault of London's corrosive climate.[66] It was to sculpture, however, that Pennethorne first addressed his inventive genius, insisting that it should be 'the most finished and most perfect work of art'.[67] The idea of producing a building with a prominent statue appealed to him most of all, and for this, a specially designed chamber or shrine appeared to be the best solution. In his submission to the Queen, Pennethorne was argumentative even before discussion had begun. He went for scale, but wanted to avoid the character of a church, as of a park building or that of a temple. He thought it might be a mausoleum, but, whatever the case, he was convinced that it should be classical.

The design he eventually submitted *was* a classical mausoleum, rather as *The Times* had suggested at the beginning, but one that was more richly decorated than is usual for the type. The building was sixty-five feet square, on a platform more than twice the size, raised seven feet above Rotten Row. There were to be sixteen statues in all, four on each front, all representing the Arts and the Sciences. Sixteen bas-reliefs encrusted the monument, portraying the main public events of Albert's earthly career. Like Donaldson, Pennethorne wanted fountains east and west of the Memorial. Very much as an uninterested footnote, Pennethorne mentioned that the cost of the proposed 'Central Hall of Science and Art', the projected, but ailing Albert Hall, would be £80,000.[68]

In fact, Pennethorne had made a sketch for an Albert Memorial, as a private initiative, soon after Prince Albert's death. He had told Eastlake of this as early as May 1862, describing his intentions as being 'without then any special object, but rather to form my own views on the subject'.[69] He shelved this while the obelisk business was absorbing the Committee and the Press, but his design seems to have been quite prophetic: he had designated that the Memorial should form a 'place' in Hyde Park, opposite the Horticultural Gardens, and that its architectural character should be dominated by a forty-foot dome covering a monumental statue of Prince Albert, formed partially out of the ideas of temple and mausoleum, although directly reminiscent of neither. Inside there were to have been marble panels with bas-reliefs and bronze statues representative – again the theme is familiar – of the Arts and Sciences.[70]

Sir Matthew Digby Wyatt's design
Sir Matthew Digby Wyatt's *Report to accompany the Design for the Albert Memorial and Institute* was privately published in January 1863.[71] Wyatt wanted of the Memorial and Institute that 'the whole shall be productive of a sensation of unity and balance in every part'[72] and, unlike Pennethorne, gave his time and attention to

both equally. The special interest he showed in the 'Institute', the early cognomen for what is now the Albert Hall, may be a recollection of the part he played, with Prince Albert, in the creation of the Great Exhibition of 1851. Charily, he insisted that 'magnificence cannot be procured without great cost.'[73]

Wyatt's own tastes would have dictated the classical style, but his political sense allowed him to consider a 'lofty Gothic memorial', particularly appropriate, he thought, when considering the character of the site. He worked out his views on both. He also sent in a design for a sculptural group, evidently not wishing to miss a single chance. *The Builder* describes his efforts as 'effective and admirable',[74] and in his own submission Wyatt claimed, as others among the architects had done, that he had 'sedulously avoided anything funereal'.[75]

Wyatt described his classic design (the drawings have disappeared), as a domed building with four porticoes, opening to reveal a colossal statue of Albert. Wyatt proposed that the lunettes enclosed by the penedentives should have scenes, painted by a special process, displaying significant scenes of Albert's life, and he further suggested that most appropriate of these would be the Prince's marriage, the opening of the Great Exhibition in 1851 and his 'habitual assistance in the Council Chamber of State'.[76] On the fourth side Wyatt wanted the lunette glazed so as to illuminate and reveal the memorial statue of Albert which was the monument's chief purpose. Allegorical figures representing Justice, Chastity, Prudence and Temperance (held to be Albert's own leading personal characteristics), would fortify the impression made by the inscription 'To Albert the Good/Great/ Royal/Wise', variously placed on each of the four sides of the frieze. Above each pediment there were akroteria, and the pediments themselves were filled with sculptures of Commerce, Science and Arts, while at the angle of the Memorial there were to be statues representing the four continents. The whole ensemble was to be of Portland stone.

Wyatt's alternative medieval design was an open octagonal shrine, enriched with sculpture and enamelled with terracotta, laid with mosaics and covered with images.[77] If Wyatt's classical design referred to the public and commercial sides of Prince Albert's life, then his medieval design, perhaps more appropriately in terms of associations, considered instead the Prince Consort's spiritual characteristics, and the statuary he proposed was to be emblematic of Faith, Hope, Charity and Mercy. The inscriptions on the frieze were to be the same as for the classical memorial, but in the spaces for decoration afforded by the octagonal plan, there were to be sculptured episodes showing Prince Albert's intelligent benevolence: typical scenes which Wyatt proposed depicted him at meetings of the British Association, at the Royal Society of Arts and, perhaps less clearly, at Trinity House.

If a purely sculptural memorial should win the day, then Wyatt had a contribution to make there as well. His proposal was that such a monument should be 'extremely simple in all its leading forms'[78] and that the subject should be a bronze sculpture depicting 'Britannia crowning the Prince with a wreath of honour'.

Wyatt estimated that his three memorials would cost £35,000, £37,000 and £25,000 respectively, but accompanying these only moderately expensive memorials there were to be fountains of National Science and National Art, where a prominent figure in a certain discipline would represent the whole body of knowledge: for instance, Francis Bacon for Philosophy, the Marquis of Worcester (who claimed to be the inventor of the steam engine) for Physics, Wren for Architecture and, significantly, Turner for Painting.[79]

Like Thomas L. Donaldson, Wyatt wanted to build first-class residential property nearby and, like all the other competitors, he was anxious that funds should not be too limited (for no grant of any kind had so far been obtained from the government) and, at a time when German architecture was enjoying a high reputation in Britain,[80] he referred to the examples of Berlin and Munich where civic generosity allowed 'continuous employment of the ablest talent in the country'.[81]

Edward Barry's design
In a manuscript submission, Edward Barry suggested that in the Albert Memorial, architect, painter and sculptor should work hand-in-hand,[82] and that white marble should be the medium chosen for their expression. A building, he said, should serve as a base for the sculpture. There is no trace of Edward Barry's drawings, and as he left a greater part of the explanation of his design to them, his proposal is not clear, although it seems that of all the architects, he attached a great deal of significance to the idea of the Albert Hall: 'the Hall itself, with the statue of the Prince, might be erected immediately and the Grand Entrance, portico and dome might be built either at once or hereafter',[83] he writes. Edward Barry's total scheme for memorial and hall, which was much less persuasively argued and presented than any of his rivals', came to a total estimated cost of £393,000, suggesting that the lost drawings have a lot to make up for over his textual description.

Charles Barry's design
Charles Barry, who had offended Scott by his interference in the Foreign Office business, thought that only two schemes – marble statues protected by a building, or bronze statues exposed to the air – were possible, and being an architect he naturally favoured the first, not least because 'an outside statue would possibly be liable to injury, either from mischief or malice, in times of popular commotion' and this spectre 'must be painful to all relations and friends' of the Prince.[84] Other arguments Charles Barry used against the idea for a monumental sculptural group were that it would be dwarfed by Kensington's trees and that, belt and braces now, large-scale portrait sculpture is, in any case, invariably unsuccessful.

Charles Barry favoured the Italian style. He said that the most appropriate architectural mode for the Memorial would be 'the peculiar and beautiful architecture' of Siena, Assisi, Pavia and Florence.[85] He cited, by name, the Certosa of Pavia as an historical model where all the arts combined in a single edifice to the greater glory of each. The design he suggested was to be of a Greek cross plan with a cupola at the crossing; the arm of the cross opposite the entrance was to be apsidal and would house the memorial statuary, placed slightly ahead of the chord of the apse: light would enter and illuminate the memorial group via the medium of stained glass. The statuary itself would have figures of Religion, Purity, Truth and Constancy surrounding Prince Albert and, on the lower part, there would be representative groups of the Fine Arts, as well as of Manufactures and Commerce. Inside, Barry continued his animated description and proposed 'British marbles of appropriate colour'.[86]

On the walls there would be panels with frescoes showing scenes from the life of the Prince, the effect being enhanced by narrative bas-reliefs. In the spandrels under the dome Barry proposed to employ the 'revived Venetian mosaic':[87] in medallions there would be figures representing the chief Christian virtues.

The exterior of Charles Barry's design (Plate 16), which sounds from his description as though it was as sumptuous a conception as Scott's, would have statues in stone and marble combined, with metal roofs and dome, *partially* gilded so that economy was not totally the victim of effect. Dedicatory inscriptions over the entrance and elsewhere in imperishable mosaic would announce the monument's purpose to those who had, somehow, failed to recognize it.

16. Charles Barry, competition design for the Albert Memorial, 1862 (*Royal Institute of British Architects*).

Charles Barry's proposal was imaginative, as well as being convincingly and closely argued. However, just to be sure that the Queen, or her advisers, should not feel he was being too dogmatic, he also appended a small scheme for an equestrian statue and a Hall to accommodate 1,800 people which would be, like his other memorial, 'not like anything else in this country'.[88] His extraordinary design, *The Builder* confirmed, could 'not be liable to be mistaken for, or confounded with, any building in common use'.[89]

George Gilbert Scott's design
George Gilbert Scott presented his *Explanatory Remarks on the Designs Submitted for The Memorial to His Royal Highness the Prince Consort and the Proposed Hall of Science* in a more attractive form than any of the others submitted by the invited architects.[90] Each page of text was boxed in red and the whole submission was bound in stiff boards.

Scott's proposal was a mixture of speculative genius, careful, scrupulous argument, a dedicated professionalism in matters of detail and a potent defence of the Goths in front of the phalanx of classicists which confronted him. He noted that:

I have felt a great perplexity as to the scale of outlay to which I should proportion my conceptions. From the time of the very first proposal of the Memorial, my thoughts were almost constantly directed to the subject.[91]

Scott used verse to describe the difficulties of his labours:

Such is the impulse and the spur he feels,
To give it praise proportioned to its worth,
That not to attempt it, arduous as he deems
The labour, were a task more arduous still.[92]

It is clear from Scott's submission that he *had* spent a great deal of time on planning and thinking on the Memorial, presumably seeing

this unsolicited invitation to compete in a national, although restricted, competition as a compensation for, if not a vindication of, his treatment at Palmerston's hands in the Foreign Office competition. It is clear that Scott attached a very special significance to the memorial project, which he considered the most important architectural enterprise of the day : as well as a personal advantage to be gained from a success, there was to Scott – and it is perhaps doubtful whether the two can be separated – a professional advantage as well : his own success in this highly-charged symbolic competition would establish with surety the Gothic as the leading style of the day.

Scott's official submission was specially careful to demonstrate his credentials as architect of the Albert Memorial. Defending his choice of Gothic, he pointed out that the public expected more than a mere group of sculpture. Besides, Scott claimed to have won the Prince's approval for the Gothic style he chose for his original Foreign Office design.[93] Scott also cited Prince Albert's approval of Gothic in his own Wellington College Chapel and Guards' Crimean Memorial designs.[94] He was ready for a fight.

Scott's Albert Memorial design, a detailed discussion of which is the subject of the next chapter, was partially based on the idea of the Eleanor Crosses, monuments which he found specially touching. He spoke of giving

. . . this over-shadowing structure the character of a vast *shrine*, enriching it with all the arts by which the character of *preciousness* can be imparted to an architectural design, and by which it can be made to express the value attached to the object which it protects.[95]

By introducing 'all the arts subsidiary to architecture',[96] including Dr Salviati's 'revived' mosaic which Charles Barry had also chosen, Scott hoped to give his Albert Memorial the feeling of completeness and preciousness – the last his own word – which he held to be essential.

In thinking about the Albert Hall, designs for which he also submitted, Scott suffered from an embarrassment of ideas, but he was inclined to favour the Byzantine, a style he felt was halfway between medieval and classical – a shrewd enough judgement considering the scholarship of the day.[97]

Scott's Byzantine design for the Hall had two domes and three monumental entrances, the fourth side being reserved for a piece of monumental statuary. Just to be sure, Scott also offered two other designs: one semi-Byzantine (and, therefore, cheaper) and one Gothic.

An undated sketch perspective of the Albert Memorial was published by *The Illustrated London News* in July 1863 (Plate 17),[98] but the other drawings, which *The Builder* described as 'magnificent'[99] appear to be lost. *The Builder*, however, maintained a diplomatic caution about historicism, even when it was 'magnificent', maintaining that there was something humiliating about architects in the nineteenth century having to search the Middle Ages for inspiration. Scott, of course, would probably have agreed, even if he would not have expressed the idea precisely like that: as time went on Gilbert Scott began to realize with increasing certainty that the style he did so much to develop was, in fact, becoming an entirely novel Victorian one, and not a revival of something long past.

The Third Report of the Prince Consort Memorial Committee was published in March 1863[100] after Eastlake, Cubitt, Clarendon and Derby had had a chance to consider the designs which had been submitted. This *Report*, which passed their judgements on to the Queen, ended the Committee's work.

By this time public subscriptions to the memorial appeal had only barely exceeded £60,000 (and Scott had already written to the Committee estimating the cost of his Memorial alone to be £100,000).[101] It was inevitable that the idea of the Albert Hall to accompany the Albert Memorial be dropped, at least until it

was revived under different and more favourable circumstances. It appears that the Queen concurred in this, being at this time anxious that nothing should prevent the speedy and successful completion of the memorial to her departed husband. This move made the work of the Committee easier: it had only to consider the designs for a memorial. It found Hardwick's design attractive for its economy,[102] but it was Scott's which won the most general approval:

. . . as especially worthy of your Majesty's favourable consideration, a magnificent design by Mr Scott, for a Gothic cross, the statue being within the structure but open to view, and in a great measure open to the air.[103]

The Committee was aware, like *The Builder* magazine, of the possible objections to Scott's peculiar brand of historicism, but did not dwell on the matter as it was felt that his design would be so original and splendid that this would 'abundantly compensate for any actual or imagined resemblance to other structures coming under the denomination of a Gothic cross'.[104] It seems that the usage of the early 1860s allowed a liberality with the meaning of 'original', but the Committee was nevertheless so swayed by Scott's design that it recommended it to the Queen, regardless of cost.

There was, in fact, some extra funding on the way: the money was found by Parliament. On 23 April 1863, the House voted £50,000 personally to the Queen and left to Her Majesty all executive power over the design of the Memorial. Henry Cole, who had been sitting with Scott in the Visitors' Gallery watching this debate, immediately telegraphed Grey at Windsor and told him that a spontaneous cheer went round the House when the money was passed.[105] Cole wrote to Grey the day afterwards and said that Scott was displeased when his design was referred to as an Eleanor Cross, instead of as a kind of spiritual derivation from that type. Cole, displaying a taste for pedantry which

eventually irritated even the members of the
Queen's household, quizzed Scott about how a
'shrine', as he wished his design to be known,
could be open to the air, when its most precious
object would be exposed to the corrosive atmosphere of London. Cole, having lost the battle of
the Industrial University, gloated over a minor
victory here in the Visitors' Gallery: Scott, he
told Grey in his letter, 'evidently had not worked
out that idea'.[106]

According to Cole's portrayal, Scott can be
imagined as a nervous and unsure type, willing
to take advice and guidance from the meddlesome curator of South Kensington. Cole tried to
influence Scott to change his design, suggesting
he did without the external decorations (the
principal part of the design which had so
impressed the Committee) while maintaining
the original proportions, but raising the height,
as *The Times* of that morning had suggested, to
300 feet. 'Your genius can do it,' Cole told Scott,
and then he wrote to Grey saying, 'And of course
he did not flinch at *that*.'[107]

A Board of Trustees was appointed to administer the parliamentary grant and the monies
raised from the appeal which began at the
Mansion House meeting. The Trustees, who
were Cubitt, Sir Charles Phipps, Alex Spearman
and Lord Torrington, had about £104,000 to
administer.[108] Cubitt died in October 1863, an
event predicted by increasing illegibility of his
handwriting, and he was not replaced.

The Royal Sign Manual Warrant, giving
permission for the Albert Memorial to be erected
in Hyde Park, was signed by Grey on 6 April
1864,[109] and the idea which *The Builder* had
dreamt of, that there should be a 'grand union
of the arts' to honour the one who loved them
so well, that they should find marbles and rich
materials fused together with the 'cunningest
art'[110] to make a fitting memorial to the hero of
family life, was closer to realization now. The
Queen was satisfied; Henry Cole was, at least
briefly, quiet, and George Gilbert Scott was
about to set out on an enterprise which was to
become the most testing of his career.

3 Scott's Design

The Albert Memorial was designed to combine the skills of the jeweller, enamellist and artist with those of the architect. Although in its early stages Scott evidently did not foresee how important the Memorial was to be in his own career, nor in the part it was to play in the development of architecture and the decorative arts in Britain, it became his masterpiece, a glittering and crocketted *summa* of the Gothic Revival and of the cultural conditions which created it. It won Scott a knighthood, although at first his attachment to it had been so casual that he did not even supervise the production of the working drawings himself; nor was he even present at some of the crucial early meetings to discuss the execution of his winning design.

An encrusted monumental shrine, housing a memorial statue and surrounded at its base and on its outer parts by emblematic statuary, the Albert Memorial is as various in its parts as Scott's own career, and as unequivocal in its expressiveness as the resolution of Scott's character. His integrity, probity and purpose are apparent in every careful, anxious letter that he wrote; Martin Shaw Briggs, his first biographer, tells us that Scott had a 'sterling character . . . remarkable talents . . . unflagging sense of purpose',[1] the last being a characteristic apparently inherited by Scott from his grandfather, the biblical commentator, Thomas Scott (1747–1821), as assuredly as Briggs borrowed the very expression from Thomas Scott's own life in *The Dictionary of National Biography*, where the man whose commentaries influenced Newman (and, incidentally, bankrupted himself and his publishers in the process) was described as having an 'indomitable tenacity of purpose'.[2]

Although his name has been synonymous with much in nineteenth-century British building which once earned righteous contempt, Scott's early career was spent in those branches of architecture most closely allied to social purpose and not in those involving radical and imaginative restoration, or pinnacled vulgarity.

Indeed, Scott's first recorded meeting with Prince Albert had been at the worthy opening of the Infant Orphan Asylum in Wandsworth in 1843.[3]

Henry Roberts, his teacher, had been an early influence on Scott's career, and although Scott left Roberts' offices in 1834 he did not immediately abandon the opportunities offered to workhouse builders by the *New Poor Law* of that year, a decision he was to look back upon with some distaste and regret.[4] However, Scott came under other architectural influences which did not have their roots in the medieval past: as a youth, he had amused himself by sketching London churches while, at the same time, he was learning the classical and academic values from a drawing instructor who had been a pupil of Sir Joshua Reynolds; he was also reading Sir William Chambers' works and studying James Stuart's and Nicholas Revett's *The Antiquities of Athens*, the pattern book of the Greek Revivalists.[5]

As a young man, Scott began to fall under the increasingly persuasive influence of Augustus Pugin, whose great trilogy had married in the informed mind the causes of social progress and beauty in the service of Gothic, or middle-pointed, architecture. Scott won his first church competition at Lincoln in 1838, and sensing that success in this was not merely luck, but an affirmation of a correct formula, he subsequently avoided the risks of variation and experimentation, and imitated his thin and mean Lincoln design in his next six churches.[6]

It was a church design, as well, which formed the central, early success of Scott's career. This was the *Nikolaikirche* in Hamburg, a project to which Scott addressed himself by entering into an earnest study of fourteenth-century German Gothic,[7] even though the winning design looks demonstrably English in Wimmel's stern north German city: it was the only Gothic entry for the competition.[8] Scott's preparation for the design was typical of the man, as was his subsequent justification of his treatment, which

assumed the character of a treatise on Gothic;
when attacked by the *Ecclesiologist* for being in
the service of the Lutherans[9] he prepared a
daunting, theological discussion,[10] which
showed him to be, in the family tradition, no
less competent a theologian than, nowadays, a
Goth.

In England it was the Oxford Martyrs'
Memorial in St Giles' which was Scott's formal
declaration that his architectural ambitions
were to be henceforth associated solely with the
Gothic Revival. This straightforward memorial
cross was built in 1841–3 as a challenge to the
Tractarians by a non-conformist group anxious
to 'celebrate' the martyrdom of Cranmer, Ridley
and Latimer, burnt in Broad Street in 1555–6.
In his design Scott had referred to his own studies
made of the Eleanor Crosses during the 1830s,[11]
but Pugin, as well as archaeological research,
was a source for Scott's Oxford design. When
still a boy Scott had admired Pugin[12] and by
the 1840s his enthusiasm stopped only a little
short of adulation. It was under the influence of
Pugin that Scott changed his character: 'A new
phase had come over me, thoroughly *en rapport*
with my early taste, but in utter discord with
the "fitful fever" of my poor-law activity.'[13]

It was at the time of this awakening that
Scott was invited to compete for the Martyrs'
Memorial competition, and although he modestly
put his invitation down to the influence of
friends in high places and expressed a scepticism
about his own talents and ability, he was
confident that only Pugin could have bettered
his design: assured in this belief, he threw
himself into the design with all the ardour he
possessed.[14]

The gulf in style and expression between the
Martyrs' Memorial and the Albert Memorial
illustrates the development of the Gothic
Revival over a twenty-year period, but Scott's
allegiance to Pugin remained unshifting. Writing
in 1869 to General Grey about the inclusion of
himself in the sculptured frieze around the

podium of the Albert Memorial, Scott revealed
the extent of his debt to Pugin:

I have chosen . . . an unobtrusive position behind
Pugin to whom I desired to do all honour as the
head of the revival of medieval architecture and in
many respects the greatest genius in architectural
art which our age has produced . . . and had it not
been for his labour it would have been impossible
to have produced such a work as this memorial . . .
not to mention that his writings have been the one
great guide to the return to truthful generous and
real principles in our art . . . my ambition, then,
would be to appear as his disciple.[15]

During the years which separate the design
of the Martyrs' Memorial and the Albert
Memorial Scott travelled widely, making
frequent journeys to France, Italy and Germany.
It was on trips such as the one he made with
Benjamin Ferrey in 1851, visiting Italy via
Berlin and Vienna, that Scott broadened his
repertoire; what is more, it was on this very
trip that he met Ruskin and David Roberts.[16]
By the time of the Albert Memorial competition, Scott was not only the most prolific of
English architects, he was also one of the best
travelled and most widely experienced.

This, however, did nothing to prevent
criticisms being made about his successful
competition design. Early on, in April 1863,
there was already some uneasiness about the
possible expense of Scott's design. Henry Cole,
forever anxious to create a new dimension in
creative interference, wrote to General Grey,
suggesting that, in view of the feared cost, the
architect be given a fixed fee of, say, £1,500-
£2,000, instead of being paid *pro rata*.[17] In the
same letter, Cole opens a window on to Scott's
personality in adding that the architect should
meet the honour-seeking, self-elected contractor, John Kelk, and not be 'jealous' of him.[18]
Scott was still feeling emotionally bruised after
the Foreign Office *débâcle* and wary of any

intrusion which might be made into those professional areas which this scion of an emerging profession regarded jealously, perhaps, as his own.

The Queen had selected Scott's design exactly as it had been submitted, but wished the architect to consider some criticisms, perhaps in royal genuflection to the various rumblings which Henry Cole was making. Grey's diplomatic talk to Scott is instructive and subtle: '. . . She by no means wishes to preclude the consideration of such modifications or changes as may on further reflection appear to you to be desirable.'[19]

Just before Scott heard that he had been selected by Her Majesty, he sent General Grey an explanatory, and somewhat cautionary, article called 'Explanatory Remarks on the Designs submitted for the Memorial to His Royal Highness the Prince Consort and the Proposed Hall of Science'.[20] In this Scott chose to defend his own architectural position. He asks whether the Prince Consort's personal taste was wholly classical, to which rhetorical question he supplies his own answer: 'No', because

when I had in the Spring of 1858, the honour of laying before His Royal Highness my first designs for the new Government offices, he distinctly told me that he did not sympathize with the objections which had been made against them on the grounds of their style being medieval – he preferred variety of style and thought the constant adoption of a single style fatiguing in its monotony.[21]

Scott claimed that Prince Albert had also enthusiastically approved his own Gothic design for a Guards' Crimean Memorial.[22]

In justifying further his lonely choice of the Gothic for the Albert Memorial, Scott wrote:

I have not hesitated to adopt in my design the style at once most congenial with my own feelings, and that of the most touching monuments ever erected . . . the 'Eleanor Crosses' . . . I would further suggest, that this style has a peculiar appropriateness in the present instance, from the circumstances that its perfect revival has been, up to the present time, the one great characteristic of the history of architecture during the reign of Queen Victoria.[23]

The precise style which Scott chose, if 'precise' is a word which can reasonably be used in so glorious a confection, was that of the thirteenth century, although treated with a certain liberality; Scott felt this age to be 'the finest period of the indigenous Architecture of the countries of Northern Europe'.[24]

Scott may have taken inspiration, in part, from Pugin's repertoire of middle-pointed detail: the front cover Pugin made for St George's, Southwark (now in St Augustine's, Ramsgate) is a prototype ciborium remarkably similar in its generalities to the Kensington Memorial. Certainly, Scott regarded other ciboria and tabernacles – the ones which overshadow the shrines in ancient basilicas, as he put it – as fitting inspiration for a memorial design. The purpose of these ciboria as prototypes was to provide decorative, protective cover for a memorial statue, acting as a vehicle which could be encrusted with decoration so that the character of the preciousness, necessary to the meaning of such an edifice, might be enhanced, and 'by which it can be made to express the value attached to the object which it protects';[25] in the case of Scott's design, the object being protected was to be, of course, a monumental sculpture of Prince Albert.

Besides drawing inspiration from certain historical examples, Scott wanted also to be 'wholly original'[26] in that his memorial design improved on its medieval precedents by being monumental in size, and therefore appropriate in scale to the majesty, both familial and spiritual, of its subject:

The object at which I have aimed is, so far as possible, to translate back again into a real building the idea which must have floated in the imagination

18. Franco Pieraccini, Orcagna's shrine, Or San Michele, Florence (*Victoria and Albert Museum, Department of Prints and Drawings*).

of those ancient shrine-makers; and to produce in reality such an ideal structure as they adopted – without ever having seen it in their minds' eye – as the models of their fairy structures.[27]

Scott was aware that not everything in the miniature shrines could be profitably translated into architecture on a monumental scale, and he was happy to envisage heavy materials like granite giving the proposed Memorial a solidity and boldness which a too literal rendering of the materials of the miniature shrines might have compromised,[28] although it was in the metalwork of the roof, gables and flèche that Scott could, in his design, imitate most exactly the ideal he had in view.[29]

Scott claimed as eclectic sources for his design the Scaliger monument at Verona, or the shrines of the Three Kings at Cologne, Notre-Dame at Aix-la-Chapelle or St Elizabeth at Marburg, or even perhaps, as Richard Redgrave suggested to Grey, Orcagna's shrine in Or San Michele in Florence (Plate 18):[30] but *The Times* was critical of the complacent domesticity of Scott's design, calling it a 'safe old English model of the so-called Eleanor cross',[31] and prophetically adding that the Memorial must be large because 'a century hence Hyde Park may be surrounded by buildings much higher than we could now imagine.'[32]

However, the most severe criticism of Scott's design came, not unexpectedly, from Henry Cole, who, as the genius of the South Kensington Museum since 1852, regarded himself as having proprietorial rights over all activities in the Kensington area. Cole's 'activity was always conspicuous'[33] and his flair for publicity brought him to occasional popular ridicule. In many ways he and Gilbert Scott make a congruent, while contradictory, character match: Cole's *Diaries* reveal something of the man, although they are hardly a window into his soul. A neat, regular hand describes, throughout 1863, the mechanical duties and obligations of a man of position who often spent thirteen hours a day at work. On

Thursday 26 February, Cole went to Windsor to see Grey; day-dreaming, he stayed on the train as far as Maidenhead. Grey showed Cole the Albert Memorial designs and the latter noted: 'Scott's on the whole preferable, very wretched figure drawing in all.'[34] On 1 March, Cole spent the day writing out a memorandum on Scott's design, a task which was to assume, for a while, an increasing significance in Cole's professional life.

Although Cole could admire Scott – he comments that St Michael's Cornhill is 'finely restored by Scott'[35] – he took particular exception to Scott's Albert Memorial design. Distressed that Grey was content to leave almost all the details of design to Scott himself, Cole sought to divert the course of development by bringing to bear on the issue all the might of his museological erudition. Pedantic, maybe; scholarly, perhaps: Cole wanted influence in the memorial design, and in order to discredit Scott and assume for himself a role of some significance and influence as an arbiter in matters of monumental, memorial taste, he published a *Memorandum on Crosses and Shrines in England* (Plates 19–21).[36]

This *Memorandum* was a calculated exercise in pedantry. Cole, in viewing Scott's design for an open ciborium type memorial, insisted that no example was known of a memorial cross not rising as a *solid structure* [Cole's italics] from its base. He added that of the original fifteen Crosses which Edward I erected to commemorate his first wife, Eleanor of Castile, only those at Geddington, Waltham and Northampton remained standing (in 1863, and they remain in 1980). He went on to say that the only crosses open at their lowest storey were common market crosses, such as those at Malmesbury, Cheddar, Chichester, Glastonbury, or preaching crosses, such as those at Hereford, Spitalfields and Leighton Buzzard. For Kemp's Edinburgh Walter Scott Memorial, Cole, like Ruskin, reserved special contempt:

Prospetto Geometrico del Celebre Tabernacolo esistente nella Chiesa di Sta in Malæta in Firenze, opera è scultura di Cosimo Seggiani
Pittore Scultore d'Architetto Fiorentino

210.

19. Malmesbury Cross, Wiltshire, autotype from
Henry Cole's *Memorandum on Crosses and Shrines
in England* (*HM The Queen*).

20. Coventry Cross, Warwickshire,
autotype from Henry Cole's
*Memorandum on Crosses and Shrines
in England* (*HM The Queen*).

21. Queen's Cross, Northampton, Northampton-
shire, autotype from Henry Cole's *Memorandum on
Crosses and Shrines in England* (*HM The Queen*).

The Edinburgh Scott monument is the only example of a Gothic canopy surmounting a *sitting* figure in the *open air*, and has the affectation of affording protection to the figure, which it does not do. It was erected at an early period of the revival of Gothic architecture; it is an admitted failure and solecism, and is an example to avoid rather than to imitate.[37]

In erudite style, Cole went on to say that those market crosses which were known to have had open sides no longer existed, while all known open shrines, such as Edward the Confessor's at Westminster or Becket's at Canterbury, were all inside buildings, and even then were much decayed by the depredations of time.

Cole's conclusion to his *Memorandum*, employing a pedantry which as previously noted irritated even the members of the Royal House-hold, was that, whatever the practical or artistic merits of Scott's design, the view from South Kensington indicated that in order that the Albert Memorial should meet the scholarly requirements of the Department of Science and Art, it should either be a proper imitation of an Eleanor Cross and stand outdoors, or it should be open, like an authentic medieval shrine, and placed inside a building. Not only were there, in Cole's view, historical and artistic reasons for the modifications he proposed to make to Scott's design, but he also held the practical objection that it was unwise to expose marble statuary to the corrosive depredations of the London atmosphere. Writing to Sir Charles Phipps[38] in May 1863, he suggested that the Queen appoint a 'Committee of Science and Art', including the Master of the Mint, Baron Marochetti, the sculptor, the Director of the British Museum and either of the architects, Tite or Smirke,[39] to solve a problem which existed only in his mind.

Naturally, Scott – who had prepared his defence against the possibility of such an attack – became anxious. The Foreign Office episode, where Scott's humiliation at the cavalier hands of Palmerston forced him to retire for three

months at Scarborough to recruit his health and confidence with a course of sea air and quinine, was going to repeat itself.[40] The circumstances eloquently revealed the delicate professional status of an architect – even a leading one – in the 1860s: with Cole's insistent interference, Scott might again be humiliated.

Scott soon sent Phipps a reply to Cole's objections, which Phipps had privately published for circulation with Cole's *Memorandum*, the better to facilitate informed discussion on the matter of the style and propriety of Scott's design. Phipps told Grey that Scott was 'evidently very much irritated about Cole's objections – not only at their matter but at their tone.'[41]

Accurately understanding Scott's delicate psychological furniture when it came to matters of professional conduct, Phipps observed:

He seems to have the greatest dread of Cole who, he says, is certain if these objections are overruled to bring forward others, and to thwart and disturb him in every way. His distrust of this overactive man unfortunately extends to Kelk [the con-tractor], who he says is a friend and employee of Cole's.[42]

Scott's reply to Cole's objections were lucid and convincing: to have a closed shrine was 'to destroy the whole idea of the monument'[43] which would then become

. . . unintelligible except by the verbal explanation that the lower story [sic] contains a room or cell in which the statue is enclosed to protect it from being soiled or injured. This seems to me highly objectionable: indeed almost destructive to the effect which such a monument should produce.[44]

In order to defuse Cole's doubts about corrosion, Scott proposed, apparently with serious intent (although nothing was to come of it) that a 'special engine' be produced 'with hose formed in a delicate and suitable manner'[45] to play water over the memorial statue of Albert, and so prevent cumulative besmirching and corrosion of the statue in the acidic London air.

Outflanking Cole in another respect, Scott moved to make his own interests congruent with those of the sculptors. He was cautiously aware that, even though he had won the competition, full executive authority was not necessarily his. He writes:

Every sculptor will be nominated by Her Majesty, and the Queen will no doubt herself give them their leading instructions. I trust, however, that I may not be considered presumptuous if I ask as the architect, and consequently as the originator of the idea of the monument, so much *influence* as to ensure our all working together as mutual coadjutors the one to the other. I would not presume to ask for *power*, – this would be assuming a higher part where all are equals; but, as the designer of the monument, I think I may ask to have an acknowledged *influence* by which the unity of the work may be promoted and its success thus rendered more certain.[46]

A little later, Sir Charles Phipps spent a couple of hours with the architect, still finding, according to his notes, that Scott was 'a good deal excited . . . and in considerable alarm for the future'[47] in considering the proportions of Cole's threat. Phipps did what he could to comfort and encourage the anxious architect, as he, in fact, found Scott's arguments a convincing rebuttal of Cole's attack. Indeed, the style of Phipps' correspondence suggests that the meddlesome Cole did not enjoy much royal favour. Phipps wrote to Grey of Scott's design, ' . . . in spite of Cole, I think more beautiful every time I look at it . . . '[48]

It was at Osborne, on 11 May 1863, that the intrusive Cole was finally silenced by Phipps, on behalf of the Queen. The official dealt with taste and materials: as far as the former was concerned, the Queen's expressed wishes made all further discussion redundant, and only expert opinion could decide on the latter.

'As regards the form of the Memorial', Phipps noted, ' . . . I should not like to enter upon a discussion which I should esteem to be closed by the Queen's selection',[49] and 'The only point that should be carefully guarded would be that the suggestions should be given and received in a spirit of abstract and impartial enquiry and not of jealousy and controversy'.[50]

Cole was silenced, but to punish him as well, Grey mischievously decided to ' . . . make Cole, as a penalty for all the trouble he has given us, have Mr Scott's remarks printed. They have their own press at the Science and Art Department'.[51]

Directly after this, Phipps ratified Scott's own position, assuring him of the Queen's confidence in his ability to carry out his great work and – a coup for the architect, this – 'In the appointment of a working committee to communicate under Her Majesty's immediate direction, the necessary executive orders, The Queen will direct the Members to leave to you full control over the works, within the limits of the available funds.'[52]

Scott was now in an officially recognized, unassailable position, while public knowledge about the results of the competition was beginning to arouse popular speculative interest. Messrs Day sought permission to publish a chromolithograph of the design; *The Illustrated London News* wanted to publish it, too (which it subsequently did, in its edition for 11 July 1863); *The Builder* had already illustrated it in its edition of 23 May 1863.[53] This last publication, in *The Builder*, so incensed Cole that although he had written to Phipps, backing down, on 12 May[54] he insisted on continuing his interference, writing to Grey again, pointing out Scott's errors in scholarship and in taste.[55] His indignation, however, had to remain righteous: in the first place by his art, and in the second place by his reasoned argument, Scott had made sure that the new Albert Memorial was, after all, to be his own enlarged, modern version of a thirteenth-century shrine. Enriched by emblematic statuary and by all the decorative arts in conjunction, it was to be a summary of nineteenth-century aspirations.

A model was soon prepared, but – despite Henry Cole's wishes – only after the working drawings had been completed by Mr Coad, Scott's 'able assistant', working under the supervision of Scott's eldest son.[56]

Both working drawings and the model were prepared just after November 1863 so that the Queen might know exactly what to expect from the completed monument. The model was placed on a pedestal in Buckingham Palace, and it was intended that critical discussion should take place. Scott liked models, and took the commissioning of the model-makers seriously; Farmer and Brindley of Westminster Bridge Road were chosen, Scott describing Brindley's soul as 'absorbed and devoted to his art'.[57] Details of the sculpture, modelled by Armstead (shortly to start his nine years' work on the podium frieze) were made in plaster and polished so that the effect was exactly like stone; details, before models and sketches had been made, were necessarily vague.

The whole elaborate business of commissioning and making the sculptural programme which so enhances Scott's architectural conception had not yet started: the model, exhibited at the Universal Exhibition in Paris in 1867, was a more confident vision of the completed Memorial than the vacillations of the sculptors, once they had begun, were going to allow over the next decade.[58]

His architectural design approved and the details, at least so far as he was concerned, finished, Scott's trials now began. By the middle of April 1864, in cooperation with the contractor, Kelk,[59] Scott had prepared an estimate of the costs. The main part of the Memorial, they thought, would cost just a little less than £66,000; the podium friezes, Armstead and Philip suggested in a separate estimate, would

alone cost almost £20,000.[60] Substantial figures, which would ultimately be far exceeded. With the beginning of the task in overseeing the production and supervising the creation of the fabric, Gilbert Scott was shortly to realize that, for a fairy structure, some of the problems he would encounter would be very substantial too . . .

4 Continents, Skills and Parnassus

The sculpture is the purpose of the Albert Memorial; all the decorative arts, combined with architecture, are there to set off either the memorial statue of Prince Albert himself, or to elucidate further the various groups of statuary whose job it is to enhance, by the agency of didactic art, the Prince's reputation as a humane bond between the continents on the one hand, and the arts and sciences on the other.

The focus is Prince Albert. He is surrounded by the sophisticated marmoreal emblems of the continents, the skills of commerce, manufactures and engineering, and the Parnassus of the fine arts, from David to Beethoven, Homer to Goethe, Hiram to Sir Charles Barry, which Victorian Britain considered to be its legitimate inheritance and the basis upon which its own arts flourished.

Gilbert Scott did not, of course, design the sculpture himself, but from the first, he was characteristically anxious to maintain a high degree of control over a scheme that was, in its generalities, his own conception. He writes:

The sculpture had been drawn out in a general way on the first elevations, partly by Mr Clayton and partly by my eldest son. From these general ideas Mr Armstead made small-size models for the architectural model, and imparted to the groups a highly artistic feeling.[1]

The architect thought very highly of Armstead's own skills as a sculptor, believing his work on the model of the Albert Memorial to be, in fact, the fullest realization of his own artistic intentions. Scott maintained that Armstead's models influenced the appearance of the completed monument; indeed, it was Scott's opinion, modified and enlarged later in life by difficult experiences with the intractable artistic temperaments of the sculptors eventually employed, that Armstead's original models were in some cases at least the equal of the finished pieces.[2]

It is certain that Scott's experiences in working with the sculptors may have contributed towards his disaffection with the original, utopian idea about the Memorial, that in it architect and sculptor should, as in the Middle Ages, work hand-in-hand in selfless harmony. This idea had for some time a considerable hold over Scott's imagination: he addressed the idea in a paper given to Leeds Philosophical Society[3], reprinted it in *The Builder*[4] and developed it frequently in private conversation and correspondence.

His argument about the unity of the arts, buttressed by material apparently acquired from James Fergusson's recent histories and from Charles Robert Cockerell's studies of Wells Cathedral,[5] spoke of uniting the sentiments of the Greek and of the Gothic, the perfection of the former being enhanced by the warmth of feeling of the latter. In the two sculptural styles he found a 'marvellous consanguinity' and in bringing the two in contact, Scott felt he saw the future of art, a vision denied to his medieval predecessors because

It so happened that at the period at which the architecture of Europe in the Middle Ages arrived at perfection, the arts of painting and sculpture had not attained the same high point . . . possibly . . . the Architectural impulse was too energetic to admit of equal perfection in painting and sculpture.[6]

Experience modified this idealism : perhaps recalling, wistfully, the excellent models of the easy-going honest workman Armstead, Scott felt he

. . . ought to have exercised a stronger influence on the sculptors than I have done. My courage rather failed in claiming this, and I was content to express to them my general views both in writing and *viva voce*.[7]

The union of the fine arts which Scott aimed at in the Albert Memorial was, he felt, exactly what the Prince Consort himself would have 'most earnestly desired'.[8] This, of course, pro-

vided the architect with a splendid royal sanc-
tion to assume some degree of overall control
over the sculptors who would be working under
him:

... though it is furthest from my wish as the
architect to assume a position as regards the other
artists engaged in that work ... I think I may ask
them so far to admit me to their counsels as to
become in some degree a bond of union between
them and to exercise a modest influence of a
suggestive kind with a view to promoting that unity
of purpose which is so essential to the success of
our common work.[9]

The sculptors to be employed were theoretically
urged by Scott to imitate neither Greek nor
Gothic styles in statuary, but to attempt a
synthesis, or the 'production of an art directly
emanating from the artist's own mind'.[10]

It was at about the time that Scott was
making public his ideas about what might be
called the theory of the Albert Memorial, a time
before neither sculpture nor sculptors had been
decided on or commissioned, that the Executive
Committee became anxious about the potential
cost of his elaborate design. Scott had wanted
written in to his contract that he should have
control over the estimates of the cost of the
architectural carving and the metalwork and,
therefore, retain overall artistic control.[11] His
own first estimate, written on Athenaeum paper,
was scrupulously vague.[12] The Executive
Committee, keen to safeguard the Queen's
interests no less than her purse, threatened
design modification to cut the cost, if no firm
estimates materialized.[13]

Scott's anxiety to retain complete artistic
control over all aspects of the Albert Memorial
at a time when neither decorative work nor
sculpture had been commissioned, was at odds
with the Committee's interest in the wealthy
contractor, John Kelk, whose offer to build the
Memorial at cost was an attractive one. As
contractor, he would influence those parts of the
Memorial which would be considered 'architecture' rather than sculpture, and Scott disliked
the idea of ceding so much power to anybody
else, especially on economic grounds alone when
artistic questions such as the nature of the
architectural carving were not even formalized.

It was General Grey, a man who was often
sympathetic with the architect, who explained to
the *arriviste* Kelk the official view that Scott
should, in fact, be allowed to 'select the parties
by whom the several portions of the work ...
should be executed';[14] this was a victory for art
over contracting, but Kelk was allowed to handle
the estimates and the details of the contracts.
Scott and Kelk were never on good terms.

The 'several portions' which Grey referred to
were those decorative parts not including the
eight large groups of sculpture which formed the
essential part of Scott's symbolic programme for
the Memorial. There were to be four groups
adjacent to each corner of the base of the
Memorial and four larger groups, symmetrically
disposed on the same axes, a little further out
from the corners of the base. These are always
referred to as the upper and lower groups, the
upper groups being the smaller.

In content, the upper groups should, according
to Scott, illustrate 'allegorically or otherwise,
the principal industrial arts and occupations'.[15]
The lower groups, as Scott himself expressed in a
letter written to General Grey on 25 April 1864,
should 'relate to the four quarters of the globe in
reference to their appearing as contributions to
the two international exhibitions'.[16] The site was,
after all, that of the Crystal Palace. In his letter,
Scott included some photographs of Armstead's
models which had so impressed him. Many of the
ideas expressed in these early models of
Armstead's were carried through to the
completed sculpture. In the lower groups the
continents were symbolized by animals. America
was not, at this stage, included because, at least
by the standards of 1864, it was by no means
clear which beast should symbolize the United

States. Only Europe, Asia and Africa were sketched.

Europe was represented by Europa and the fabulous bull, while 'nations' and 'races' were gloriously confused in a well-meaning imbroglio of emblematic good intentions. England and Germany represented the Teutons, while France and Italy stood, sculpted, to represent 'those of Latin origin'.[17] Asia presented more subtle and complex problems: '. . . a female figure on an elephant – unveiling herself as alluding to the great position she took in the exhibition of 1851.'[18]

Africa was also represented by a female figure, on a lion, said to represent the Ancient Egyptians, as few contemporary Egyptian paragons or negroid exemplars came immediately to the mind of a sculptor searching for emblems in the 1860s. A Nubian and a negress were shown, but only in their capacity as tokens 'intended to idealize the River Niger and the Nile'.[19]

Despite Scott's frequent and earnest pleas about architecture being the bond of unity between the other, more imaginative, arts and that, continuing the reasoning, the architect should therefore be the final overseer of all works associated with the Albert Memorial,[20] it was the Queen who chose the sculptors of the eight upper and lower groups, even though the whole artistic conception had been Scott's alone.

For the monumental statue of Prince Albert she chose Baron Marochetti, an *opera buffa* parody of the capricious artist; for the lower groups, Gibson, Theed, Foley and Bell; for the upper groups, Noble, Macdonald [sic], Thornycroft, Durham and Lawlor.[21]

All these individuals were invited to send in designs and the chosen ones were to 'put themselves in communication with Mr Scott'.[22] Of those originally selected, the Queen charitably favoured Thornycroft because of his presently impoverished state, while, despite the invitation, she had no very high opinion of either Noble or Durham, even though both 'had executed most popular statues of the Prince',[23] those at Liverpool and at Newcastle.

By 14 May 1864, the choice of sculptors had been further refined, perhaps following some persuasive and well-informed advice from Sir Charles Eastlake. Now, John Gibson was given Europe; J. H. Foley, Asia; Theed, Africa; John Bell, America.[24] Of the upper groups, Patrick Macdowell was given Manufactures; William Calder-Marshall, Agriculture; Thomas Thornycroft, Commerce and Lawlor, Engineering.[25]

General Grey wrote each sculptor a standard commissioning letter saying that every group 'will consist of five human figures, animals or such other emblems as you should think most appropriate'.[26] Small clay models, on a scale of one-and-a-half inches to a foot were to be completed by the end of October 1864, which gave the sculptors five months to prepare designs for the Queen's final approval. General Grey included a photograph of the Memorial with the standard letter, as well as suggested plans and dimensions for the different groups.

From Rome, Gibson was the first to decline the commission. Forty-six years in the climate of the Eternal City had made him unwilling to exchange it for the climactic and professional perils of a major royal commission.[27] Eastlake immediately suggested Patrick Macdowell as a replacement for Gibson on the Europe commission,[28] replacing the vacant Manufactures commission with Henry Weekes. Macdowell promptly accepted.[29] Save for the matter of organizing the podium frieze of a modern Parnassus, the business of commissioning the sculptors was virtually over.

Before proceeding to a more detailed study of the individual statues, it may be useful to say a word about the character of Victorian sculpture. By the 1860s, sculpture had arrived at the stage when its purpose was to be the plastic suggestion of an idea that was primarily literary, not visual. If realism was proffered instead of idealism, the latter was preferred. In all fields of sculpture there was, at this time, a mania for detail and a dogmatic insistence on moral rectitude, only occasionally modified by the iconographical changes encouraged by political expediency.

With severe moral certainties, much obscured a century later while we consider them, the conflict between fact and sentiment was debated. Decorum and allegory were in advance of either genius or inspiration when a sculpture had to be considered. An individual sculptor at work on a group could expect to be in the process of long, dutiful and careful amelioration, according to the generalized prejudices of his judge and assessor.

The insistence on literal truth led to absurdities which, comic now, seemed then merely to enhance the delicious excitement of experimental art. Not least of the causes of these absurdities was the fact that literal truths could not always be universally *read* when rendered in stone. John Bell, campaigning in 1872 for explanatory inscriptions to be placed around the base of his sculpture of America, the better to aid the comprehension of a sluggishly responsive public audience, illustrated the problems of too strict an adherence to a literary programme. Looking back, he told the story of how, while he was chipping away at one of the faces of America, a US Army General, called Key, happened by and, taking an intelligent interest in sculpture, introduced himself and

... after saying some polite things about the group, added 'but there is one thing in which you are quite wrong' and turning me round to Mexico said 'this is not in the least the character of a North American Indian'. When however I explained that it was not so intended, but for a Mexican or a Central American he was quite satisfied with it. I understood that Mrs Lincoln the widow of the late President made a similar remark and I don't wonder at it![30]

John Bell, with a conviction lost to artists today, felt this episode indicated a flaw in the General's perceptions. Such was the character of mid-Victorian sculpture and its sculptors.

5 The Unstained Princely Gentleman

Scott's own drawings (Plates 22, 23) show that his conception of the central statue of Prince Albert had always been that the princely gentleman should be shown seated, in regal dignity, even though this chosen posture did excite some controversy among the squeamish about the delicacy of the position, when viewed from below.[1] He had also wanted the statue to be carved in stone, but when he inspected the condition of the Sicilian marble on Marble Arch – and saw it sadly deteriorated – he became more than ever aware of the problems of exposing marble in London's corrosive climate and, suspecting that if the proper moves were made, an official donation of bronze might be forthcoming, he shifted his taste towards bronze as the medium of the statue of Albert.[2] That was in July 1864.

The Queen's chosen sculptor, the headstrong Marochetti, had always considered bronze to be the most suitable material for rendering plastic his own elevated thoughts about statuary, and, in particular, about Prince Albert. This material also had the incontestable benefit, in the sculptor's view, of being more expensive than marble and, therefore, more productive of a beneficial percentage for himself. He wanted £10,000 to do it, and he wanted the money immediately.[3] Because no bronze figure of a similar size had ever been attempted in London, it was difficult for official adjudicators to argue with Marochetti's estimates, even though they were twice what Scott had suggested they might be.[4] Of the £10,000 Marochetti had so quickly demanded, he was promised £3,000[5] and started work, or, at least, appeared to, soon after 15 July 1864 when the commissioning letter sent by Sir Charles Phipps in fact arrived.[6]

The niceties of capturing in sculpture the complex geometry of Prince Albert's character were tantalizingly challenging for a Victorian sculptor devoted to the pursuit of continuously elaborated allegory and the finer distinctions of decorum. Fanny Aikin-Kortright's fragrant retrospective prose captures the saintly mood exactly.

While he lived, half that was noble and exalted in his nature seemed unobserved, or at least unappreciated; it was not till the tomb had closed upon the blameless Prince that his image rose before us – once the virtuous man . . . the promoter of the best and wisest social ameliorations, the encourager of art and science, beyond all, the exemplar of an unstained life . . Vice was banished, or at least abashed.[7]

Before attempting so daunting an artistic task as capturing in bronze this prodigy of virtue, Marochetti had to face some rude realities, a confrontation for which his extravagant personality did not well equip him. There were contractual conditions to be met, against which his elaborately contrived artistic temperament could rebel. The sitting figure of the Prince was to be fifteen feet, three inches tall, on a base of ten feet, nine inches by nine feet, dimensions settled by Scott as the module for both the upper groups showing the continents as well as for the central statue of the Prince.[8] The Baron was bound to produce two models, a smaller one (for which he would be paid £1,000) and, if Her Majesty approved, this would be worked up into a full-size one (for which he would be paid the further £9,000) to be tried for effect on Scott's pedestal.[9]

The royal bureaucrats were scrupulously anxious that the Queen's interests should be protected, a caution maintained out of all proportion to the actual risks which the Royal Household exposed itself to in the undertaking. In case of the death or the illness of the unfortunate sculptor, for instance, the Queen wanted the models to become her own property so that, against so tragic a sudden demise, the models would not become lost in the confusion of the contest over the artist's will. This would enable the Queen to get the sculpture cast by

22. George Gilbert Scott, sketch of the Albert Memorial (*HM The Queen*).

23. George Gilbert Scott, sketches of upper and lower groups and of the statue of Prince Albert *in situ* (*HM The Queen*).

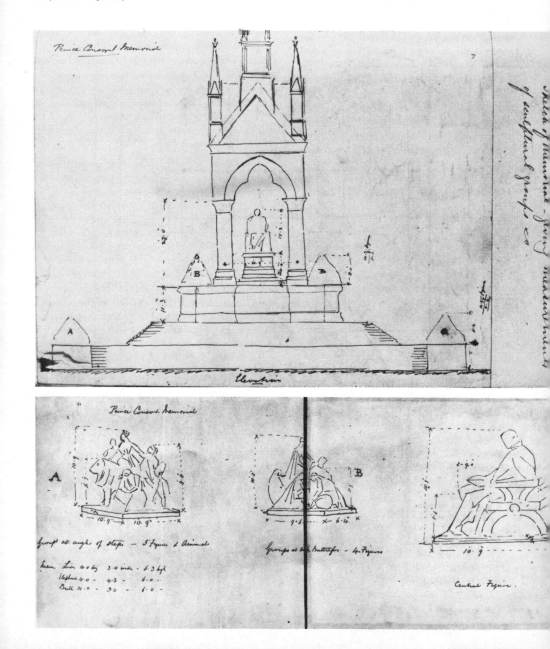

whomsoever she pleased. Faced with this, Marochetti capriciously demanded the retention of full artistic control over a project into which he had, in any case, invested very little artistic energy. Without the total freedom his spirit demanded, he would cease work (in fact, before he had begun).[10] This arrogance on the behalf of a foreign artisan-artist brought a strong reaction from the members of the Royal Household: General Grey promptly suggested that William Theed be given the commission as an alternative and less troublesome sculptor, while Sir Charles Phipps wrote an embarrassed letter to the *sui disant* Baron telling him the commission was to be taken away from him (even though, all the while, Phipps – who had no artistic judgement – had personal doubts, thinking that if Marochetti *were* the best sculptor available then he should be allowed to work on his own terms).[11] The threat of withdrawing the commission brought a rapid response from the sculptor: in an access of artistic pride and economic humility, he promptly declared himself willing to execute the statue for nothing, but still rejected the suggestion that any part of the manufacturing process should be taken out of his hands.[12] A new agreement was made on 12 July 1865.[13]

By spring 1867, Marochetti – having apparently settled down to his commissioned task – had finished a fourteen-foot plaster model which had been inspected by Scott and Layard.[14] They were only moderately impressed, and then not favourably, being somewhat overwhelmed by the blinding effect of so large a mass of white plaster when seen in the strong light of a small studio on a bright day. Prudently, they suggested it should be cheaply gilded to make it more attractive before the crucial inspection by the Queen.[15] Marochetti captiously pronounced himself to be displeased with the views of Scott and Layard and, with that attention to ameliorative detail already

noted, the Baron promptly fashioned a new head for his monumental statue.[16]

On 1 May 1867, in conditions of considerable secrecy, Scott and Marochetti studied the draft statue *in situ* on the Memorial's pedestal. Each acknowledged that the presence of the scaffolding did little to improve the apprehension and the appreciation of the sculpture, but that alone, it was determined, could not account for the singularly unhappy effect of Marochetti's art upon the viewer: 'somewhat too large' was Scott's own reserved opinion and it was, therefore, suggested that its size be reduced by one-tenth.[17] Layard, despairingly, suggested that the drapery be lightened.[18] The grumbling Baron, quick to interpret a criticism of his weak art as a covert criticism of the inadequacies of the brief, now proclaimed that he had always wanted to produce an equestrian statue.[19] To Scott, this naturally seemed a ludicrous suggestion, in the context of the character and proportions of his shrine,[20] although both Sir Edwin Landseer and Henry Cole, when called upon to advise, felt the Baron's suggestion to be a sensible solution to the perceived problems.[21]

Scott simply did not like Marochetti's design, but tact informed his response as he was always aware that his own position remained, perhaps, slightly tremulous. He wrote to Layard that:

I did not feel when the model was placed in its position, that the difficulties arising from the sitting position were the main causes of the defects which we perceived to exist.[22]

In the same letter, after drawing attention to the ugly, massive limbs which distinguished Marochetti's design, Scott took off on an eloquent attack on the incongruities of the mooted equestrian statue, a tirade so persuasive that the immediate results were that the Queen instructed General Grey to tell the Baron to concentrate on the existing brief[23] and *The Daily Telegraph* printed a critical report on Marochetti and his materials.[24]

Criticism spurred the Baron on to merely providing another model of his Prince Albert statue design, but mechanically reduced (as Scott had suggested) by one-tenth; when the architect inspected it at the Royal Academy in August 1867, he was prompted to observe that the idle sculptor had made no real effort and, suggesting Marochetti to be acting out a plot of reflexive spite, that he had 'no wish for it to succeed'.[25] The petulant sculptor tinkered further with the statue, suggesting now the robes of the Garter, now a Field Marshal's uniform, but never being willing to reappraise his own design.

Gilbert Scott was sensitive to arrogance, to self-interest and to mischievous negligence. In Baron Marochetti he found exquisite variations on all these qualities and consequently announced himself to be in despair at the prospect of having to deal further with the slothful, intractable sculptor. The further to confound the father of the Memorial, Marochetti, adopting a yet untried psychological posture, even suggested that another sculptor be commissioned.[26]

Weeks later, the petulant Marochetti was demanding a further £1,000 on the outrageous grounds that 'it is not my fault if there are alterations to be made,'[27] thereby putting himself higher on the helix of increasing official disfavour, and approaching day-by-day the moment when his bluff would be called and another sculptor commissioned in his place. The complex layers of administration surrounding the Albert Memorial suited Marochetti's negotiating techniques entirely: he would write to one member of the Royal Household, argue with Scott, and then make complementary claims upon another member. Employing this technique, he had managed to extract a part of the supplementary £1,000 he had demanded from Sir Charles Phipps (immediately before the latter's death), a fact which, had Layard not

discovered it in time, would not have prejudiced the Baron's further claims for advance instalments of his fee. General Grey maintained a fastidious dislike of Marochetti, finding him 'very disagreeable . . . to deal with',[28] and it was he who first brought up the name of John Foley as a possible replacement for the Albert statue commission.

The discontent with Marochetti was general. Layard, holidaying at the Hôtel Bonivard at Chillon, undertook to call into the Baron's Paris studio on his return trip to London; in the meantime he declared himself 'by no means at ease about Marochetti's work',[29] but cautiously advised that to take the commission away from the fractious old man would do serious damage to his artistic reputation, a charitable consideration not then uppermost in Grey's mind.

When other sculptors discovered the problems Marochetti was having in satisfying official taste, there was a modest sense of urgency to supply a more fitting work for this major commission, unblemished by procedural problems and fashioned by the agency of their own genius. The most pressing and consistent claim for consideration in this respect came from John Bell, already engaged as sculptor of the America group. Bell thought that Marochetti was 'singularly wanting in artistic knowledge',[30] at least compared with himself, and he frequently wrote to General Grey, telling him so. Criticizing other designs by the unfortunate Baron, Bell accused him of making castings deliberately complex so as to increase costs and, therefore, to increase his own returns, *pro rata*. He also said that elements of a certain recent Marochetti commission 'would really disgrace the cheap statuary shops in the Euston Road'.[31]

Marochetti died in Paris on 29 December 1867, an event which might even have been stage-managed, for maximum effect, by the sculptor himself. His demise did little to lessen the problems with getting the central figure of Prince Albert finished promptly, but it was an efficient cause of official relief among the courtiers hitherto responsible for ministering to the eccentric sculptor's daily caprices. The Keeper of The Privy Purse, General Thomas Biddulph, made a gesture more practical than sensitive in immediately asking whether the Committee was obliged, by the terms of the late sculptor's contract, to pay his descendants, his own disinclination to do so being stimulated by the fact that Marochetti's model had never been officially approved.

Marochetti did not leave behind him a happy popular reputation, and the Queen had to appoint Lord Stanhope and the Director of the British Museum, W. Newton, to see if there was any of the Baron's work which was worth salvaging.[32] The answer would have been perfectly clear in the public's mind; *The Kensington News* (a journal often critical of the Memorial as a whole) reported that Marochetti had become

The butt of every wit and satirist in Europe, his composition wrecked his fame, and – so popular rumour has it – killed him by the crushing influence of failure upon a sensitive mind.[33]

With salvage in mind, after a visit to the Baron's studio, Lord Stanhope succinctly reported that he did not find the model of Albert clad as a Field Marshal appropriate to a celebrated practitioner of the Arts of Peace,[34] tastefully failing to report to Her Majesty the intelligence that Marochetti had devised a statue of the nude Prince from which to work up his designs.[35] It was felt that no self-respecting sculptor would be prepared to take over where Marochetti had left off,[36] so when it was suggested to the Queen that Layard should formally approach John Foley about taking over the commission, the Royal reply was 'certainly, without delay'.[37]

Foley's terms of contract were established in May 1868 and were tight enough to obviate any repetition of the Marochetti *débâcle*. He was bound to complete the bronze statue within two years, at a fee of £10,000 which was to include the costs of casting and gilding.[38] The bulk of his payments were to be held over until he had completed the statue and had it in place on Scott's pedestal, so that – with the shades of Marochetti present – satisfaction could be guaranteed, at the expense of the artist.

By August, Foley had made some sketches, some showing Albert in an armchair, others showing him regally disposed on a stool. Everyone considered these a 'very great improvement on Marochetti's design'.[39] Layard preferred the stool, but the royal preference seemed to favour a Gothic chair, upon whose chief characteristics Scott was invited to advise.[40] The design showed the late Prince Consort leaning forward '. . . as if taking an earnest and active interest in that which might be supposed to be passing around him.'[41]

Despite the acclaim which Foley's early sketches acquired, with no statue yet tangibly ready to fill the void in Scott's design, there was an opportunity for ambitious sculptors to press their own claims in providing a central figure of Albert. John Bell was egregious amongst contenders. He proposed his three-and-a-half-foot model of Albert as a Soldier of Christ, kneeling 'although not fully perhaps' – a subtlety this – 'in the act of prayer' (Plates 24, 25).[42]

Bell felt that Scott's insistence on a seated figure was, with that love of bizarre, exotic precision so characteristic of the age, better suited to Greek, Roman or Italian architecture. He was prepared to consider as alternatives to his kneeling design either a recumbent or an *Assunta*- like figure, rising transcendent heavenward, baulked only by the obstructive architecture of Scott's Gothic canopy, but on the whole he disliked the sepulchral character

24. John Bell, sketch for statue of Prince Albert as a Christian knight (*HM The Queen*).

25. John Bell, model for statue of Prince Albert as a Christian knight, contemporary photograph (*HM The Queen*).

they might suggest.[43] An equestrian statue, rather as Marochetti had whimsically hoped for, was also dismissed on the grounds that the horse would not fit, given the conflict between the laws of natural scale and the hieratic requirements of having a statue of Albert sufficiently monumental in size.

Despite a vigorous campaign to get John Bell's Soldier of Christ adopted as a replacement for Marochetti's unhappy model – a campaign supported at various times by General Grey, John Clayton and Fanny Aikin-Kortright throughout the neglected pages of *The Court Suburb Magazine for Objects of Suburban Interest and General Literature*[44] – the industrious, if slow, Foley continued work on his officially approved task. When he called to check on the sculptor's progress during late June or early July 1869, Layard commented that the likeness which Foley had contrived was a happy one and that the whole effect which was produced gave 'that life to the figure which was so much wanting in Baron Marochetti'.[45] A few weeks later, Foley prepared a sketch and placed it in a model of Scott's canopy, so that the effect might be judged, and Layard found this 'very satisfactory'.[46]

It was planned to place Foley's full-size model on Scott's pedestal on 29 June 1870,[47] and it was estimated that casting would take a further eight to ten months. It must have been fairly difficult to judge the effect of the statue when the model was tried in place, because the Memorial itself was then barely complete: its south and east fronts were finished only as far as the upper granite cornice, while the west and the north fronts were not even that far advanced.

These trials with Foley's models encouraged John Bell to continue his campaign of criticism against the idea of showing Prince Albert sitting down. In private correspondence he maintained his stand, the more heartfelt and desperate now that the possibility of realizing his own scheme was becoming daily less likely. He claimed that Foley's statue must be rethought because '. . . a gilt seated colossus indeed were more than an aesthetic and artistic error – it would be a political mistake,'[48] and although Bell did not amplify this gnomic point, his campaign was aided by a sharp-tongued correspondent in *The Kensington News*. With a sense of destiny, Bell started styling himself a 'kind of male Cassandra',[49] as being the only one blessed with the vision to see the error of the official ways. He continued his campaign throughout 1871, even getting so far as to produce a standing alternative to his original kneeling design.[50] Prepared to try anything to win attention for his own design, Bell even went as far as quoting from Fergusson's *Handbook* a passage about stability, suggesting to Scott in March 1871 that the central figure of Prince Albert be replaced by a central structural support, thereby leaving four open niches which could be filled by statues of the Prince in different stages of his career,[51] a design solution which may even have been suggested to Bell by the example of the sculpture on the polygonal faces of the Eleanor Crosses themselves. Bell's continuous hectoring for his own design to be considered, especially when he knew well that Foley's commission had been given by the Queen, did nothing to endear him to the Executive Committee. A campaign of prejudice against a brother artist, at a time when progress on his own America group was, to say the least, slow, prompted the remark from Doyne Bell that

. . . if he had devoted more time and attention to his group and less to his pen we should not now be receiving the unfinished work which he is tardily erecting on his pedestal.[52]

Foley's own leisurely progress – 'we may see the statue in 1873'[53] was a remark muttered here and there – was caused both by his declining health and, perhaps more relevantly,

26. Steel engraving of J. H. Foley, Prince Albert, from Dafforne's *The Albert Memorial*.

27. J. H. Foley, Prince Albert (*Photo: Ben Johnson*).

ALBERT

by his absorption with the temporarily more beguiling statue of Lord Canning. After Foley's model statue was raised on to Scott's pedestal in 1870 it remained there until spring 1871, in preparation for being cast in bronze from thirty-seven old guns which were moved into his studio in January 1872.[54]

By late 1873, when W. Newton and Doyne Bell[55] visited Foley's studio, they found the head already moulded and cast, with the large model which had stood on the pedestal cut in many places, the legs and arms then being in the process of moulding.[56] The assemblage of this colossal statue – which had 1,500 parts – was felt to be one of the most complex ever attempted,[57] a further complexity being added when Foley died unexpectedly in 1874, after succumbing to pleurisy, a complication brought on after catching a chill at a window during a wedding party;[58] however, because the statue was substantially ready for casting there was no great difficulty in completing the work, and Foley had left instructions that T. Brock, his assistant for nine years, should complete the work in the event of his demise.[59]

The process of completing such a sculpture in the nineteenth century should not be under-estimated. Art took a back seat to technology and mechanics. For instance, Marochetti left behind him a cornucopia of equipment, redolent of a dockyard: two crane ladles, a blowing machine, sand grinding machine, numerous presses and clamps, a lifting jack, a cast iron blast furnace and an overhead traveller and gantry.[60]

Foley left behind parts more artistic than mechanical, but still presenting operational problems for his inheritors: half-finished casts and various dismembered parts of Prince Albert's statue littered his studio. Doyne Bell reported in July 1875 that the two larger portions of the body were in the sandpit, being welded together, but for an undisclosed technical reason, this operation could only

proceed eight inches at a time. Afterwards the limbs would be welded on and the plinth placed on the pedestal, but raised on blocks two feet from the ground so that when the main portion and the head were lowered on to the plinth, the parts could be screwed together, the workmen could withdraw and the whole could then be finally lowered on to the pedestal.[61] Then the completed statue was to be covered with a canvas box so that the gilders, adding the final glittering touch to the statue, could work undisturbed.

By October 1875, Prince Albert, unstained, but yet ungilded, was complete, and Weekes and Armstead, the sculptors who had been appointed referees on Foley's death, approved him (Plate 27).[62]

By the time the gilded Prince, pensive and holding the catalogue of his Great Exhibition, was revealed to the public, the rest of Scott's structure was tarnished, and excited speculation about the character of the Memorial statue had congealed into petulant indifference. The contrast between the gilt Prince and the grubby shrine provided a displeasing contrast which reminded *The Daily News* that 'It is . . . impossible to ignore the general hostility provoked by the colossal statue.'[63]

Had Marochetti's statue ever been completed on time it might have caught the public imagination at the peak of a wave. As it was, Foley's gilt colossus merely looked out of place. By 1875 Prince Albert was a memory and the statue, although given some attention during the First World War when the gilding was removed during the salvage drive, has remained ignored from that day to this. *Ars brevis, vita brevis.*

6 Parnassus

One hundred and sixty-nine inhabitants of a High Victorian Parnassus have been frozen around the breezy podium of the Memorial of the nation's great loss. The execution of such a Faustian task was the most splendid sculptural aspect of the Memorial: the podium on which Prince Albert squats is encrusted with all mankind's eternal geniuses of the fine arts, suggestive of the timeless basis upon which the arts in England presently flourished or, at least, as they were supposed to: in fact, despite the superficial cornucopia of artistic expression in mid-nineteenth-century England, it was widely realized that the visual arts, at least, were in need of encouragement or revival. For instance, Sir Charles Eastlake had published an essay, as early as 1848, the intention of which was to revive the English School of history painting.[1]

Armstead's and Philip's massive marmoreal historiography is not unique in Europe. Indeed, it was a characteristic of European art at this time to attempt to classify and organize the past in a meaningful Whig manner so that the present condition of the arts might the better be accounted for. Paul Delaroche's mural painting in the Hemicycle in the Amphithéâtre of the Ecole des Beaux Arts in Paris (1836-41) is the relevant familiar prototype, where sixty-six artists from classical Greece up to the age of Louis XIV are grouped on either side of Ictinus, Phidias and Apelles, before antique architecture and beneath the blue vault of heaven. Delaroche had depended on his own taste for the criterion of selection,[2] and although Armstead and Philip were subject to more stringent procedures, being under the control of an executive committee and subject to guidance from their scrupulous architect, it seems likely that the whole scheme was, however remotely, influenced by that of Delaroche.[3]

The idea was, of course, originally Scott's, although he gives away little about his inspiration. More so than other of the sculptures,

the podium reliefs came under surveillance by the architect and the Executive Committee. It was the contemporary feeling that

This, taken as a whole, is perhaps one of the most laborious works of sculpture ever undertaken . . . each figure not cut, as is usual, out of a detached block, so that every portion can be easily perched and the waste stone readily struck off, but – on the contrary – hewn, or, more properly, *excavated* out of the solid mass of the Monument.[4]

Scott was particularly concerned about the selection of the stone, considering it a 'subject of considerable anxiety'.[5] The Sicilian marble he had originally specified was found wanting in terms of durability in the London climate, but a Chantry statue which Scott inspected was found to have a surface like sandpaper only forty-five years after its completion.[6] Istrian marble was dismissed because supply was unreliable, and, in the end, aided by the merchant, Fabricotti, Scott settled for Canpanella marble (that is, it sounded like a bell), a type rarely used in England,[7] and one whose hardness was eventually to cause Armstead and Philip considerable difficulties in execution.

It was in May 1864 that Scott first wrote to Grey, asking him for his opinion about the position of each group – Painters, Musicians, Poets, Architects, Sculptors – on the various sides of his hectodecahedron.

The arrangement Scott proposed (Plate 28) was that Architects should be on the north side, Sculptors on the west, Painters on the east and that Poets and Musicians should share the south side.[8] Scott believed that this arrangement, with Solomon as the centre of the Architects, and David as central figure among Musicians and Poets (a religious touch suggested by Dr Harley), embodied the very idea of the Memorial:

My idea in the arrangement suggested [in his plan] is that it avoids selecting either of the three com-

28. George Gilbert Scott, plan of sculptures on the
Albert Memorial, 1867 (*HM The Queen*).

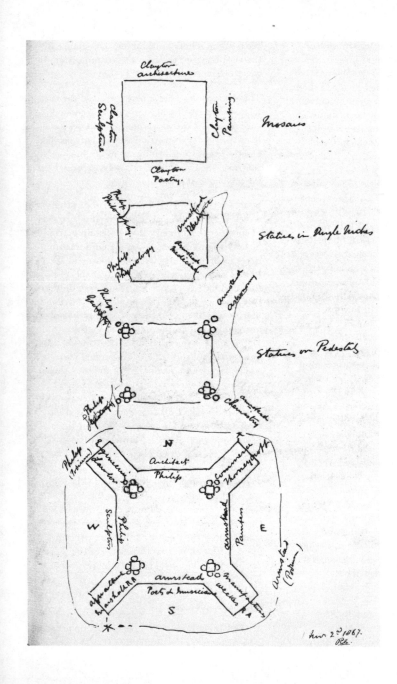

monly received fine arts (I mean Painting, Sculpture and Architecture) for the foremost place – but it places Painting and Sculpture on the two flanks united in front by Poetry as their *ideal* bond of union and by Architecture behind as their material bond of union.[9]

The Poets and Musicians on the south and the Painters on the east were the work of H. H. Armstead, the sculptor-modeller so much admired by Scott; the Architects on the north front and the Sculptors on the west were the work of J. B. Philip,[10] a less well-known artist who was to turn out to be a somewhat troublesome character.

Both sculptors made a small model, one-twelfth scale, to test the general content and arrangement of their parts of the frieze; then a full-size model was made up from which the marble could be cut, and it was this model that was transferred to the base of the Memorial so that the sculptors could labour *in situ*.

By the end of November 1864, Armstead was writing to Doyne Bell, explaining that he had prepared a detailed description of his sculpture, but he was hesitant about Dr Harley's suggestion of placing King David in the centre of the Poets, favouring, as he did, a secure figure in the form of Homer, rather than a divine one in the person of David, as the chief among Poets and Musicians.[11] In this atmosphere of confusion Sir Charles Eastlake was commanded by the Queen to advise on all artistic matters relating to treatment of the frieze, a position he was eminently suited to take, as he could number among his own acquaintances many of the figures on it.[12]

The general strategy which was produced by the sculptors *independently* (somewhat to Her Majesty's annoyance) was that the Poets, Musicians and Painters, Armstead's south and east sides, were grouped in geographical schools, with, for instance, the Italian School symbol-ically in the centre of the Painting side and the British and German on one side, and the French and Spanish on the other. It was felt by Philip that Sculpture and Architecture were more susceptible of chronological interpretation than Poetry, Music or Painting, and he arranged his groups accordingly: 'the primary source from which these two arts was derived seems to have been Egypt', the country from which we have the earliest evidence of 'regular civilization'.[13]

In every field, the selection of artists to be displayed on this breezy Parnassus was sometimes extraordinary, often partial and always very revealing for the student of historiography,[14] posing all manner of problems of selection, interpretation and treatment for the sculptors, who, although they received considerable assistance, both solicited and unsolicited, appear to have been primarily responsible themselves for the precise choice of the heroes of culture they portrayed.

The Poets and Musicians on the south side (Plates 31-4) contain some unexpected figures, bearing in mind the state of musi-cological research during the 1860s: Handel and Weber might be expected, but Monteverde (sic) and Palestrina are, perhaps, less obvious choices, Sir Henry Rowley Bishop still less obvious.[15] From the south side the first figures to be completed were Goethe, Schiller, Bach and Handel, the sculptor Armstead, in this respect, at least, showing a loving dedication to the German School and simultaneously winning Doyne Bell's warm approval for the despatch and energy with which he carried out his commission.[16]

Armstead took special trouble with the details. His notebooks (Plate 29) are preserved in the Royal Academy and eloquently betray his concerns and enthusiasms: he attempted a Dante inkstand, essaying the familiar brooding figure there, and collected engravings of obscure portraits of familiar folk: an engraving of Arne, with a pencil sketch; a steel engraving of Hanffsmann's portrait of Bach, Waldmueller's

29. Leaf from H. H. Armstead's sketchbook showing studies for the podium frieze (*Royal Academy of Arts*).

and Letronne's of Beethoven. Horace Vernet was photographed, Armstead's drawing enhancing the original in giving considerably more lift to the painter's moustache. For his portrait head of Goethe, Armstead wrote to the German's old friend Crabb Robinson, seeking advice about minute details of the polymath's physiognomy.[17] Eighteen months later, Doyne Bell took a 'Mr Benedict' to Armstead's studio: he had known both Mendelssohn and Beethoven well, but could add only a little from personal experience to the sculptor's creative apprehension of Weber's death mask which Doyne Bell had already carefully procured for him.[18]

Layard had not been impressed by the artistic culmination of this trawl for detail: when he visited Armstead's studio, in company with Scott, during February 1866, he was more struck by the effect he noticed of 'meanness' and 'stringyness'[19] in, shall we say, Goethe's limbs in the full-size models; the shock of finding the poet with feet of gristle blinded him to the perspicacity of Armstead's physiognomic research. Yet Doyne Bell, on the other hand, found the figure of Beethoven 'most admirable',[20] an opinion echoed by the Queen and, therefore, guaranteed to win the artist favour.[21]

Armstead also grouped his Painters (Plates 35-8) into national schools. It is indicative of taste that Rembrandt is the only Dutch painter resident in the artists' heaven (Vermeer not yet having been discovered and Hals, Hobbema and Ruisdael thought inconsiderable); El Greco is missing from the Spanish School (Murillo being then thought more estimable), Piero della Francesca is missing from Italy.[22] Armstead continued his obsessive love of physiognomical verisimilitude in taking his version of Hogarth's head to the National Portrait Gallery, wrapped in a towel, so that he could adjust the modelling with reference to the terracotta bust of the painter in the Gallery's collection,[23] a process for which facilities were

denied him in reference to his capturing of Giotto's features.

It was the Architects and the Sculptors, Philip's work on the north and west fronts, which were to prove more controversial. Layard, when he had visited both Armstead's and Philip's studios with Scott in February 1866 had been critical of both sculptors, but the more so of Philip.[24] He detected professional jealousy between the two men, who were reluctant to consult one another; in particular, he found Philip's modelled heads were 'without character or expression', an effect apparently worse than having mean and stringy limbs.[25] Writing to him to tell him so in March 1866, Layard recommended that Philip needed better models and that, specifically, he should study the British Museum's statue of Mausolus, then under the care of his friend, Newton, and Enrico Quirino Visconti's *Iconographie ancienne, ou recueil des portraits authentiques des empereurs, rois et hommes illustres de l'antiquité*, an enormous two-volume book of plates of Greek and Roman busts and medals,[26] written to envigorate French portraiture.

Philip's arrangement of Architects (Plates 39-42) begins at the north-west angle, with anonymous Egyptians and the Assyrians, and then progresses chronologically.[27] Philip found an advantage in starting from a common centre, and moving chronologically, as there was created a 'harmonious junction' with the friezes of Sculpture and Painting, their points of contact being congruent in date and, therefore, in costume. Nevertheless, Philip's selection troubled him somewhat: he found it difficult to weigh and sift rival claims for inclusion between equally meritorious candidates. He noted:

I have endeavoured to include all representative men, though many, for want of space, have been omitted, whose excellence would entitle them to be added to the catalogue I have made.[28]

The nicest problem of selection which Philip had to consider was whether to include Scott among the Architects. It was Philip's inclination to do so, but the architect was afraid that it would expose him to hostile criticism from jealous rivals. Scott felt Pugin should stand for himself, and Philip, unconsciously describing Pugin's greater achievements in theory than in building, noted:

Mr Pugin was . . . a very skilful and conscientious designer of gothic ornaments [sic] and architectural details – but he can scarcely be classed amongst the great architects of this country – and having left any great monument with which his name is connected [sic].[29]

Entering into this debate, General Grey made it known that the Queen insisted that Scott's figure be included,[30] Scott being forced to reply that

My reasons for declining were, in the first place that we had limited ourselves generally to deceased professors of the different arts, and secondly that I felt it to be presumptuous to allow myself to be reckoned among those who are selected as the representatives of Architecture, and immodest, were I worthy of such a place, to assume it myself in a work under my own guidance.[31]

As the Queen had commanded it, Scott could only concur, but demanded a 'humble and inconspicuous position',[32] which wish he was granted by being shown in low relief just behind his mentor, Pugin (Plate 42).

In November 1870, Professor Donaldson was asked for his opinion about the selection of Architects: he ventured to suggest that the composition might be improved by including about a dozen other architects, saying, with some prescience, considering the taste of the time, that:

. . . Soane, Elmes, Wilkins and Smirke have erected first rate buildings and are hardly (scarcely)

inferior to Barry, Cockerell, Pugin. Percier and Vicomte and Hittorff are great names in Paris of the present period (but deceased). Stüber of Berlin was known to HRH the Prince Consort, as was also (I think) von Klenze of Munich.[33]

A little later, a correspondent wrote to *The Builder* wondering why Soane, Schinkel, Perrault, Masuccio II and Vitruvius had not been included[34] and this, it should be recalled, at a time when Philip Webb's Red House was already more than ten years old.

Philip's selection of Sculptors (Plates 43-5) went along the west front of the podium.[35] It says something of how little progress has recently been made in the study of sculpture to note that of all the other sides of the podium frieze, Poets, Musicians, Painters and Architects, it is the sculpture side which appears to modern eyes to need least revision to bring it into line with contemporary taste. That does not mean that Philip was without his problems. His progress was slower than Armstead's: by May 1865 only twenty or so of his figures were roughed out in the nude, ready to be draped[36] and, furthermore, his work was constantly meeting with official criticism, at least in comparison to the benign response to Armstead's industry, art and diligence: at the time when Armstead already had five figures emerging out of the stone on the podium, the tardy Philip was only just erecting his studio in the Park.[37]

Several official actions hindered the progress of both sculptors, a decision being made during 1868 to increase the depth of the relief from twelve inches to fifteen inches, putting them both out of pocket and forcing a change in technique,[38] but Philip was specially hindered by criticism. For instance, Newton, the Director of the British Museum, took exception to some of the sculptor's classical details:

. . . you give a representation of the Parthenon . . . in one half of the Eastern pediment . . . a composition purporting to be the representation of one of

30. The Albert Memorial *c.* 1870, with H. H.
Armstead's and J. B. Philip's sheds in place
(*National Monuments Record*).

the original compositions of Phidias . . . which
seems to be borrowed from Stuart's Athens II, pl.
VI. This composition is utterly at variance with all
that we know of the composition . . . I told you that
I objected to it very strongly . . . [and] . . . nothing
would induce me to consent to its remaining.[39]

Newton, helpfully, suggested complete erasure,
a course of action which he felt would reflect
the archaeological uncertainty. Philip's refusal
either to acknowledge or to reply to Newton's
letters aggravated the Museum Director's
already critical response to the sculpture: he
noted, also, a 'very objectionable female figure'[40]
which he would be glad to see removed, but was
eventually forced to bring all the dreadful weight
of his pedantic scholarship to bear on Scott, in
order to get a response from Philip. Scott felt
Philip had acted 'reprehensibly'[41] although this
judgement appears to have had little influence
on the sculptor's manner and manners.

The progress of both sculptors on the frieze
was erratic: it was meant to be complete at the
same time that the four upper groups of
sculpture were to be put in place, that is by
early 1870, although even the helpful Armstead
merely said that all he could promise would be
to do it as soon as possible.[42] In February 1872,
Doyne Bell was still writing to the sculptors,
requesting that they remove their studio roofs
from beneath the Memorial as soon as possible
so as to accelerate the unveiling of the whole.[43]

Both Armstead and Philip were working
under financial difficulties. In March 1870 Scott
had found them both in a 'state of chronic
depression'[44] – a not unusual condition for
artists tied to a fixed-price contract – and he
was anxious lest this financial anxiety would,
as he feared, quench any artistic fire that
remained. In reporting on the progress of the
podium frieze Scott adopted a kindly and
sympathetic tone, stressing to Doyne Bell that
both had, in fact, been working for six years
without any remuneration, delays and increased

costs having being incurred by their making their estimate before the full extent of the design was known and their using a specially hard marble which had resulted in the work being 'utterly unproductive in realizing any income whatsoever'.[45] Doyne Bell replied to Scott:

... the Executive Committee have every desire to lighten the very arduous and difficult task which these sculptors have undertaken ... but the committee are compelled to act with extreme caution in carrying out the task which has been assigned to them by HM The Queen . . .[46]

The attitude of the Executive Committee seems to have been, why pay the sculptors more when they were, in any case, contractually hooked: Doyne Bell did, however, make some concessions to the sculptors' financial circumstances: when writing to the contractor about the raising and fixing of Marshall's, Weekes', Thornycroft's and Lawlor's upper groups, he told Kelk that the Executive Committee and not the sculptors should bear the cost of the alterations necessary to their temporary studio roofs, under which they toiled while the operation took place.[47]

A problem with the efficacy of didactic sculpture no less acute than John Bell's with his America group, was whether the individual figures in the podium sculpture should be named by incisions in the stone. Doyne Bell was merely concerned whether it might add to the cost, speculating that it might, perhaps, have been in the original contract and that, therefore, no extra cost would be incurred.[48] Scott liked the idea of having inscriptions because the practice had medieval precedents, besides which, he cautiously noted, not even a polymath would be able to recognize, on facial characteristics alone, figures so diverse as, say, Ludovico Caracci or Anthemius of Tralles.[49] Scott advised that you could get letters seven-eighths of an inch tall (so small because large

lettering had a 'vulgar air') and gilt for about £60,[50] a figure apparently economical enough to win the Executive Committee's approval. Yet before the approval was given, with characteristic caution, the lists of the names which the sculptors had produced were submitted to Messrs Newton, Scharf and Donaldson, who were considered the highest authorities in sculpture, painting and architecture, so that the most accurate and distinctive nomenclatures could be found for this extraordinary monumental part-work of Victorian cultural confidence, financial stringency and artistic neglect.[51]

32. Steel engraving of H. H. Armstead, Poets and Musicians, podium frieze, from Dafforne's *The Albert Memorial*.

33. H. H. Armstead, Poets and Musicians, podium frieze: detail (*Photo: Ben Johnson*).

34. H. H. Armstead, Poets and Musicians, podium frieze: detail (*Photo: Ben Johnson*).

35. H. H. Armstead, Painters, podium frieze
(*Photo: Ben Johnson*).

36. Steel engraving of H. H. Armstead, Painters,
podium frieze, from Dafforne's *The Albert
Memorial*.

37. H. H. Armstead, model of Painters for the podium frieze (*Royal Academy of Arts*).

38. H. H. Armstead, Painters, podium frieze: detail (*Photo: Ben Johnson*).

39. J. B. Philip, Architects, podium frieze (*Photo: Ben Johnson*).

40. Steel engraving of J. B. Philip, Architects, podium frieze, from Dafforne's *The Albert Memorial*.

41. J. B. Philip, Architects, podium frieze: detail (*Photo: Ben Johnson*).

42. J. B. Philip, Architects, podium frieze: detail showing George Gilbert Scott (*Photo: Ben Johnson*).

43. J. B. Philip, Sculptors, podium frieze (*Photo:
Ben Johnson*).

44. Steel engraving of J. B. Philip, Sculptors,
podium frieze, from Dafforne's *The Albert
Memorial*.

45. J. B. Philip, Sculptors, podium frieze: detail
(*Photo: Ben Johnson*).

7 Skills

The improving idea of *industrial art* was inseparable in the Victorian mind from the equally high-minded idea of social utility: both were elevated abstractions prevalent wherever men of affairs exchanged views. The four upper groups of sculptures on the Albert Memorial depict, with distinctions we today perhaps find too fine, these industrial arts: Agriculture, Manufactures, Commerce and Engineering. The capitalization is contemporary with the idea itself and goes back to May 1864 when Gilbert Scott suggested the layout (Plate 46) with Engineering at the north-west corner, Commerce at the north-east, Agriculture at the south-west (happily closest to the Royal Horticultural Society Gardens) and Manufactures at the south-east.[1]

These subjects provided rich opportunities for the collision of fact and sentiment, the latter more often coming off better. Scott, a fairly practical man, would have preferred to have seen some greater emphasis put on fact by the chosen sculptors, but they found that concentrating on sentiment provided finer opportunities for the free operation of their varied skills as well as offering, so long as their ideas remained abstract, plenty of room to manoeuvre in areas they had themselves defined.[2] The sculptors chosen for the industrial arts groups were William Calder-Marshall, RA, to do Agriculture, Henry Weekes, RA, to do Manufactures, Thomas Thornycroft to do Commerce and John Lawlor to do Engineering.[3] Although Thornycroft and Weekes had good reputations, the one having executed an equestrian statue of Albert in Halifax in 1864[4] and the other having made the first portrait bust of Victoria after her accession,[5] the earnestness and application which might otherwise have informed progress on the upper groups of sculpture was rather impaired by the presence among the artists of John Lawlor, the sculptor of Engineering, whom Walter Strickland describes as a witty,

genial, handsome figure with a fine baritone voice, cautiously adding, however, that 'in his profession he was irregular, working only when necessity compelled him'.[6] Even though Thornycroft's and Weekes' status as Academicians was some guarantee to the Executive Committee of regularity of behaviour in the past and of the likelihood of probity in the future, Lawlor was from the start a seat of trouble among the sculptors of the upper groups.

The four were commissioned in June 1864 and each, with more confidence than was ever subsequently displayed, undertook to have a small model ready for the inspection of the Executive Committee by August of that same year.[7] While each sculptor's estimate of his costs was different, each showed a curious certainty and precision: Thornycroft maintained that four figures would cost £3,200; Lawlor ominously suggested he could do it for £2,350.[8]

The models were ready on time. Calder-Marshall originally chose to make plastic the passage from Isaiah which says 'In the Sweat of thy face shalt thou eat bread', and which became generalized into Science directing Agriculture[9] by the utility of Her learning. Henry Weekes, similarly, chose to show how Geometrical Science enlightens Manufactures,[10] while Thornycroft showed Commerce to be the agent which introduced civilization into hitherto uncultivated and barbaric nations[11] (a conceit which Scott found a 'far too complicated and artificial idea'[12]). John Lawlor, vague as to his intentions even at the beginning, showed figures consulting about a plan, one holding a handscrew (Plates 47-50).[13]

The Executive Committee viewed these models without much enthusiasm. Doyne Bell wrote a Memorandum during November 1864: he found Calder-Marshall's model of Agriculture the most satisfactory; his arrangement which contrived to leave only three out of

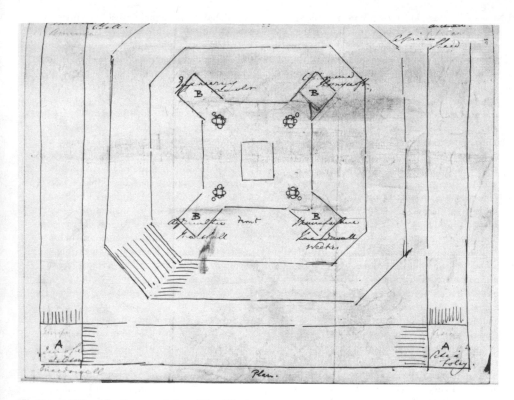

46. George Gilbert Scott, ground plan of the Albert
Memorial (*HM The Queen*).

any four of the figures visible at any given
moment was held to be particularly impressive;
Weekes' model of Manufactures was found to be
'unpleasant . . . in every direction' while
Thornycroft's model of Commerce 'overlooked
the chief medium of commerce in all ages: the
ship'.[14] For Lawlor's Engineering model were
reserved the most special opprobrium and the
most thunderous abuse. Doyne Bell:

Mr Lawlor's group I cannot but consider a signal

failure . . . the central figure is far too lack-a-
daisical to indicate the precision and firmness
which are the chief characteristics of Engineering.[15]

Discouraged by the trawl from this first
campaign of model-making, Doyne Bell
enjoined all the sculptors to consult with Scott,
fons et origo of the Memorial idea as it stood, to
see whether under his direct inspiration they
might produce some better results. Eastlake
agreed with Doyne Bell, finding his Memoran-

dum 'contains many most judicious remarks and criticisms'[16] and, again, the influential Director of the National Gallery was called in by the Queen to mediate between herself and the sculptors and, thereby, stimulate Art by his Learning. The Queen, keeping possession of the sculptors' original models, returned to each photographs she had had made of their efforts, so that some reference would be available for them in comparing their early errors with the ameliorated developments from them.

The problem with the upper groups was not just the usual one of confused allegory; most of the models were also found wanting in the more purely technical aspects of art. Of the four, Eastlake had found Calder-Marshall's and Thornycroft's the more satisfactory: Lawlor and Weekes were too short on mass and simplicity and, in his view, too extravagant in their use of fore-shortening.[17] Lawlor's effort was so widely considered weak that even Princess Louise commented on it, and Eastlake privately doubted whether the sculptor had any skill at all as a practical artist.[18] Scott's own response to the models was no more enthusiastic: generally, he was uneasy about the amount of the allegorical content and specifically, he was critical of Weekes' group for being too complicated, and of Thornycroft's for being too *sentimental* (and requiring a literary explanation), while Lawlor's was simply 'not a pleasing group'.[19] The architect's idea was that in each group the central symbolical figure should represent the particular Art or Science involved, and not an abstraction of that idea.[20] At a loss to know what else to do, Scott suggested that each upper group sculptor should be given a model of the whole pedestal so that his concept could evolve in harmony with the unavoidable facts of the Memorial: the Queen smartly took up this suggestion.[21]

Amended models were ready by March 1865, and Scott found that there were still criticisms to be made.[22] Weekes' Manufactures

was not found 'generally good', while Scott was not sure whether he did not prefer the original model of Calder-Marshall's Agriculture to the revised version.[23] Thornycroft's Commerce he now found an 'agreeable group and finely modelled, but not easily intelligible'.[24]

The kindest thing the good-natured Scott could find to say about the wretched Lawlor's efforts was that he 'professes a natural inaptitude for minute modelling',[25] venturing that the full-size version might look better, and heuristically suggesting that Lawlor might wish to visit an actual engineering works 'for the purpose of gleaning hints which may tend to render his representation more perspicuous'.[26]

The amended model of Calder-Marshall's group was approved, while Weekes had only now to cover up an outstanding naked female shoulder and Thornycroft had to replace a martial column in his group with a symbol whose more peaceful allusions would be consonant with Albert's character.[27] Two years on, in 1867, when Layard visited his studio he did not in fact find Thornycroft's group at all satisfactory, the figure of the Turk being 'especially commonplace',[28] but generally, apart from Lawlor, the other groups advanced satisfactorily from 1865.

By April 1868 Calder-Marshall (who had met with least official criticism) had finished his group.[29] Weekes had completed Manufactures by April 1870 and was asking for the money[30] which was being held back to help pay the costs, as the contractor demanded, of raising the groups on to the pedestal, a course of action (devised to avoid embarrassment) which Doyne Bell later realized to be so parsimonious as to prompt a declension into the Executive Committee's actually volunteering to meet the contractor's costs.[31]

By the time all the upper groups were published in the *Art Journal* in May 1871 the worst was over. Even Lawlor's troublesome design was complete.

47. William Calder-Marshall, model for Agriculture, contemporary photograph (*HM The Queen*).

48. Henry Weekes, model for Manufactures, contemporary photograph (*HM The Queen*).

49. Thomas Thornycroft, model for Commerce, contemporary photograph (*HM The Queen*).

50. John Lawlor, model for Engineering, contemporary photograph (*HM The Queen*).

Engineering (Plates 51, 52) included the genius of that industrial art dominating the group, with one of her hands resting on the cylinder of a steam engine, while before her a youth, as in the model, refers to a plan, and a navvy – a figure which Newton, searching for something to say, found specially successful[32] – sits to one side, opposite another figure holding a cog 'as indicative of the development of the engineer's art by means of machinery'.[33] At the back of the group Lawlor, with vast negligence of the possibilities and restraints of his medium, chose to represent a steam-hammer and a blast-furnace together with depictions of the Britannia and Menai Bridges, all held to be contemporary triumphs of engineering. While admiring the navvy, Newton had found on his visit to the artist's studio during March 1870 that the genius of Engineering was 'most unsatisfactory, bad in design and coarse in execution' and noted that 'Mr Lawlor did not seem conscious of its defects'.[34] Newton also found that Lawlor's carving was roughly executed; the left arm of the genius was not properly fixed and, furthermore, an arm of the navvy – the best figure – was fractured by careless workmanship and handling.[35] Inspecting the statue *in situ* in November 1870 Doyne Bell and Newton found the surface of the marble stunned and impaired all over by 'careless and unskilful execution' and patched up, here and there, with crude cement.[36]

Thornycroft's final efforts (Plates 53, 54) fared only a little better than Lawlor's. He placed his genius of Commerce on a column, 'this indicating, in the antique manner, her connection with navigation'.[37] In her left hand she holds a cornucopia 'showing the abundance which her counsels provide',[38] while with her right hand she encourages a young merchant, emblematically equipped with the emblems of barter: a balance, ledger and purse; the group is completed by two figures, the one bringing corn

and the other an exotic merchant holding a casket of jewels, alluding to oriental luxury.[39] When Doyne Bell and Newton were on their gingering-up tour of November 1870 they found that the genius of Commerce had an unsatisfactory joint on her right arm and that the wrist of the young merchant had a fracture where water might lodge and, ultimately, cause frost damage,[40] with the unhappy possibility of the hand dropping off.

Symbols and emblems flourished too in Henry Weekes' group of Manufactures (Plates 55, 56). The genius points to a beehive, an emblem of industry, while holding an hour-glass in one hand to show the significance of time in manufacturing operations. She is surrounded by figures representing a smith, a weaver and a potter, each of whom exhibits to her their productions, the smith being the leader as it is through him that 'arise the chief means by which the others work'.[41]

Finally, there was Calder-Marshall's Agriculture (Plates 57, 58), the group which had consistently fared the best of all, even though it was said of its creator that he had 'no more poetry, or fancy, or classic perceptions than a cow',[42] a criticism perhaps appropriate to his role as sculptor of his particular group. His sculpture shows the genius of Agriculture, crowned with a wreath, directing the attention of a husbandman at her feet from his primitive plough to a steam cylinder and cog, illustrative of the benefits which Technology might bring to husbandry. Similarly, a retort lying on the ground suggests the improvements which Chemistry might bring to Agriculture: the resulting abundance is shown by a gleaner with an armful of corn. The other branch of Agriculture, the one that involved the breeding and rearing of cattle, is tactfully represented by a shepherd boy carrying a lamb.[43]

These over-complex sculptures by under-paid artists completed the immediate surroundings of the Prince Consort.

51. Steel engraving of John Lawlor, Engineering, from Dafforne's *The Albert Memorial*.

52. John Lawlor, Engineering (*Photo: Ben Johnson*).

53. Steel engraving of Thomas Thornycroft,
Commerce, from Dafforne's *The Albert Memorial.*

54. Thomas Thornycroft, Commerce (*Photo:
Ben Johnson*).

COMMERCE

55. Steel engraving of Henry Weekes, Manufactures, from Dafforne's *The Albert Memorial*.

56. Henry Weekes, Manufactures (*Photo: Ben
Johnson*).

57. Steel engraving of William Calder-Marshall, Agriculture, from Dafforne's *The Albert Memorial*.

58. William Calder-Marshall, Agriculture (*Photo: Ben Johnson*).

AGRICULTURE

8 Continents

The major part of the sculptural programme of the Albert Memorial was completed by four large groups, mounted on diagonal axes at the outer limits of the monumental design. The timetable for production of the artists' models and the deadline for their inspection was the same as for the upper groups.[1] These *continental sentiments*, to paraphrase Scott, were to be Europe, Asia, Africa and America, the idea being of 'representing allegorically the quarters of the globe, with reference to the Great International Exhibitions which have done so much for art',[2] and, one might add, had also done so much for Prince Albert, and *vice versa*.

After the podium frieze, these sculptures of the continents were considered the most important commissions in the gift of the Queen for the sculptors. So much so that, despite being engrossed enough in the business of creating his part of the podium frieze, it seems that H. H. Armstead was interested enough to work up, in private, some models of Europe and Asia, preserved in images in his notebooks in the Royal Academy (his Asia looking remarkably like the final, commissioned version) (Plates 59, 60). Yet it was four other sculptors who were chosen to do the continents: Europe was assigned to Patrick Macdowell, an Irish sculptor who, despite his status as an Academician, never achieved anything like commercial success;[3] Asia to John Henry Foley, a grocer's son who rose to the first rank among British sculptors;[4] Africa to William Theed and America to John Bell, this last sculptor being mentioned by Rupert Gunnis as the single one responsible for bringing Victorian sculpture into disrepute, an achievement he stimulated in the production of much of his later work which all fell into 'bad taste and sickly sentimentality'.[5]

In a joint letter written from The Athenaeum on 14 June 1864, the four continental sculptors accepted their commission[6] and so much were they from now on to identify themselves with their allotted groups that, on occasions, they would in future sign their official correspondence 'Asia', 'Europe', 'America' and 'Africa', although it is by no means clear whether this formality endeared them to the Queen's officers and servants.[7]

The operating conditions for artists in the 1860s were such that with their acceptance of the commission came demands from the sculptors which they were scarcely justified in expecting to be entertained: the four made it clear that the 'colossal animals' which were to be the chief emblem of each continent would cost more than each eight-foot tall human figure, and that for these they had been offered only £800 (noting that Parliament had recently voted £17,000 for the lions in Trafalgar Square); their demand was for £3,000 each over three years for the preliminary model, with the completed piece in Sicilian marble promised at the end of the fourth year.[8] Grey thought each group should cost not more than £4,400, whether in marble or in bronze; Scott's more generous estimate was £5,500.[9]

These financial claims were justified by the sculptors in view of the *difficultas* they so enthusiastically envisaged in a joint statement they made:

Groups of this character with four fronts which should look well on all sides are without precedent in this country, nor do we remember any example of ancient art extant, that approaches them in size or complication.[10]

By 15 August 1864 the marble had been chosen and was available for inspection, slightly incongruously, in Scott's office.[11]

It remained now for the sculptors to decide on the precise treatment of their monumental groups, although the general idea had strongly been established (Plates 61–4). Foley's Asia was to be placed at the south-east angle of the pedestal: his proposal of 4 October 1864 was based on some ideas Scott had presented in

59. H. H. Armstead, sketch models for the
Continents (*Royal Academy of Arts*).

60. H. H. Armstead, sketch models for upper and
lower groups (*Royal Academy of Arts*).

April of that year; India unveils herself atop an elephant,[12] 'the prostrate animal typifying the subjection of brute force to human intelligence',[13] the unveiling of the sole female figure being an allusion to that continent's important display of products which had figured so prominently at the Great Exhibition of 1851.[14]

Patrick Macdowell decided to represent Europe according to the traditional legend, with the mythological Bull as the central emblematic colossal beast. In Macdowell's proposal we find 'Great Britain and France predominant as conservators of Peace'.[15] It was Macdowell's original intention that France was to hold a sword in one hand, sharing in the other an olive branch with England (but after it was pointed out that this symbol of Peace might be too temporary an allusion for a permanent sculpture, and it was further added that an olive branch does not work well in stone, this was changed, and signalled first by a pencil correction, to a 'wreath of glory').[16] The genius, Britannia, was originally to be represented as an 'Ocean Queen', resting on a Lutheran Bible, looking towards Germany 'from whom she has received it'.[17] Britannia's trident was to be emblematical of Sovereignty over the sea.

Germany and Italy, reflecting contemporary political preoccupations, were given rather less space in the European composition. The former, by the time the *Handbook* appeared in 1872, was described as 'the home of literature and science until the influence of Prussia brutalized her culture'.[18] Italy was intended to be shown sitting on a broken column, an emblem to signify her former greatness, to which melancholy recollection the modern genius' thoughts were now directed, a conceit emphasized by 'her hand resting on the bust of one of her emperors, while she is looking hopefully to the future', an idea which Eastlake considered to be 'hardly intelligible'.[19]

The idea of William Theed's Africa sculpture, was intended, by the juxtaposition of civilization against barbarism, to contrast the present with the past. Africa presented the nicest of all problems to a sculptor intent on doing his duty by his own art and his own colonial civilization (a dual obligation not always happily fulfilled), Theed being all the time aware that in the dark continent it was true to claim that 'the oldest states of antiquity gave an impetus to science'.[20] His model showed a female genius of Egypt (ancient) sitting astride a lion[21] while, 'surprised in his warlike costume the heathen kaffir is listening to the dictates of Truth'.[22] In due course, the better to accumulate telling details – which Eastlake found to be the most, perhaps the only, admirable aspect of his art – Theed got in touch with the Duchess of Northumberland, who lent him a dromedary saddle brought from the East by her dear late Duke, upon which the sculptor could model the saddle on the back of the camel which in the later version of the group replaced the more savage lion as the symbolic colossal beast of Africa.[23]

For his America group, John Bell decided to adopt the motto 'Advance' as being indicative of the 'progress of the human race in that quarter of the Globe'.[24] Significantly, with the United States and Canada at the forefront, the two figures at the rear were 'also advancing, but not so rapidly':[25] they represented Central and South America.[26]

Towards the end of November 1864 the sculptors had to move their models to Windsor for a Royal inspection. Eastlake found Foley's Asia a 'work of real excellence'[27] and Bell's America and Macdowell's Europe 'quite safe in their general arrangements'.[28] His strongest criticism was reserved for Theed's Africa group, on the grounds of the sculptor's inability to provide a general view, and that the whole concept lacked essential breadth and simplicity. He hoped, however, that the stimulus of Foley's 'glorious' work near at hand would be refreshing to all the other sculptors and encourage them to

61. J. H. Foley, model for Asia, contemporary
photograph (*HM The Queen*).

62. John Bell, model for America, contemporary
photograph (*HM The Queen*).

63. Patrick Macdowell, model for Europe,
contemporary photograph (*HM The Queen*).

64. William Theed, model for Africa, contemporary
photograph (*HM The Queen*).

enhance their own art with the aid of local genius.[29]

Soon after Eastlake had inspected the models, Scott inspected them too. He was a little unhappy that the utopian collaborative harmony he had initially envisaged had not worked out in practice, at least not so far.[30] However, casting some doubts as to the perspicacity, to say nothing of the veracity, of official procedures, it was exactly this collaborative harmony which Doyne Bell perceived and praised.[31] Scott noticed that Foley used traditional costume, while Macdowell and Bell relied, none too satisfactorily, on the persuasive power of symbols.[32] The architect generally approved of Asia and Europe, but doubted the usefulness of the symbolic effect of the wreath which England and France were to share.[33] Like Eastlake, Scott did not much admire Theed's work which, he thought, seemed to

. . . deviate essentially from the idea adopted by the other three. It goes off too much into sentiment, forsaking simple and readily tangible fact ; then falling into the defect which pervades modern sculptured groups, of needing a showman for its explanation.[34]

The problems with the models, then, were, as far as the architect Scott was concerned, too much 'extraneous sentiment' (by which he meant obscure allegorical references) in the Africa group ; the America group had its figures too imprecisely defined, while the suggested unity of England and France in Macdowell's Europe group was not justified by contemporary political reality. It was Doyne Bell who expressed this most thoroughly when he wrote that, taking away the wreath of glory from between England and France would, in fact, be emblematical of 'the wide gulf of thought, feeling and habit which separates the two countries'.[35] The model of Africa had conceptual shortcomings, too, not least the feebleness of the lion's paw,[36] or the unduly optimistic figure of the Kaffir, apparently enlightened by missionary enterprise in Theed's sculpture to a higher and more exalted degree than the known facts from Africa would allow.[37] Only Foley's Asia, at this stage, enjoyed universal acclaim.

Eastlake and Scott met the sculptors of both the lower and the upper groups at Buckingham Palace, just before Christmas 1864, when the official and the royal views were passed on. Theed promptly set about making considerable alterations, while John Bell's proposed modifications to meet the criticisms did not inspire confidence in either Scott or Eastlake :[38] eventually, Bell's America was to be the most testing of all the sculptural groups.

Eastlake's criticisms of Bell's group form one of the most elaborate discussions of decorum in nineteenth-century sculpture.[39] Eastlake objected, for instance, to the martial implications of the shield of the United States and, citing Creuzer and Winckelmann, suggested that Bell employ instead a classical *caduceus*.[40] With some propriety, Bell objected to the assumption of a pagan symbol for a Christian state[41] but to all Eastlake's acutely pedantic criticisms he replied with good humour and won approval for his willingness to take extra trouble with detail, going so far as to borrow real maple leaves and a beaver skin from Sir Edmund Head, the better to render the details on his personification of Canada.[42]

Amended models of all the sculptures were approved in March 1865, Doyne Bell reporting that Foley's required no change, Macdowell's needed merely to have a number of literary emblems by the side of Germany reduced, Theed's new camel which Eastlake had insisted upon needed a little remodelling, while Bell's America was required to shift the weight from one foot to the other.[43]

When Eastlake inspected the amended models he too found that Foley's needed no change, but he felt for reasons that were not explained that the female personification of Central and South America should be replaced by male figures.[44] Looking at the models, *The Athenaeum* found all the other groups so weak that it said the whole lot should be done by the estimable Foley.[45] Indeed, Eastlake found the whole business of dealing with the individual sculptors so enervating that Grey had to claim that the Director of the National Galley 'would . . . be much disheartened if he had to re-open the discussion with them.'[46]

Foley made the most rapid progress, his quarter size model being almost complete by April 1866, the sculptor wanting only a good Asiatic model to complete his iconography of the continent.[47]

Foley's expeditious enthusiasm was not infectious. In March 1869 Macdowell, Theed and Bell – all still unfinished – were writing mournfully to Doyne Bell, indicating that they were feeling the pinch, quoting fees which once Chantrey and Gibson had received for their sculptures in their own day.[48] Entirely characteristically, Doyne Bell refused them extra payment and the sculptors hammered on.[49]

As the groups neared completion, details were all the time improved and enhanced. Foley's Asia (Plates 65-7) now incorporated an Arab, perhaps included after a suggestion of Layard's,[50] with a Koran; Theed's Africa (Plates 74-6) had, alongside an Egyptian and a Nubian, a negro 'representative of the uncivilized races of this continent' who was listening to the teachings of a European female, while 'broken chains at his feet refer to the part taken by Great Britain in the emancipation of the slaves'.[51] Of all the lower group sculptors it was John Bell's America (Plates 68-70) with 'Mexico rising from a trance, and South America equipped for the chace [sic]' while Canada 'attends them, pressing the Rose of England to her breast',[52] which was most festooned with allusive details: bison, grizzly bear skin, Indian totems (the grey squirrel and the humming-bird), a beaver for Canada, a lone star for Chili (sic), volcanoes for Mexico, alpaca for Peru, a Southern Cross for Brazil, while 'in the rear, aroused by the passage of the bison through the grass, is a rattlesnake'.[53]

The integrity of Bell's artistic intentions may be judged from an account of the following incident: just as he was finishing off the group, an assistant dropped a mallet on to the United States and broke off the ever-green oak wreath of that country and the left hand which held it: Bell was quick to take the best advantage of this unfortunate incident and modified his statue so that it no longer embodied this divisive symbol of the southern states.[54]

65. Steel engraving of J. H. Foley, Asia, from
Dafforne's *The Albert Memorial*.

66 & 67. J. H. Foley, Asia (*Photos: Ben Johnson*).

68. Steel engraving of John Bell, America, from Dafforne's *The Albert Memorial*.

69 & 70. John Bell, America (*Photos: Ben Johnson*).

71. Steel engraving of Patrick Macdowell, Europe, from Dafforne's *The Albert Memorial*.

72 & 73. Patrick Macdowell, Europe (*Photos: Ben Johnson*).

74. Steel engraving of William Theed, Africa, from Dafforne's *The Albert Memorial*.

75 & 76. William Theed, Africa (*Photos: Ben Johnson*).

9 The Higher Life and Soul of the Memorial

The upper reaches of Scott's fairy structure are encrusted with an extravagant wealth of decorative and sculptural detail, composed with fanatical determination; much of the accumulated richness is scarcely visible, still less intelligible, by a viewer on the ground. It is this very degree of elaboration of detail and materials which does so much to give the suggestion of richness to the Memorial, a richness which in size, scale and degree far exceeds the medieval models which were Scott's distant prototypes. The positive effect of this decorative scheme is that the Memorial gives off an air of almost velveteen complexity and density; one negative aspect that it also gives off is an air of fragility which so troubled General Grey that he even suggested to an astonished Doyne Bell that the whole Albert Memorial be put under glass, a proposal which was prudently declined on the grounds that it might appear to be an implicit acknowledgement of physical and aesthetic weaknesses in the design.[1]

It was Scott's view that, apart from what he called the works of 'high art' (by which he meant the major pieces of sculpture), the roof and the flèche (Plate 77) were the very soul of the Memorial 'and its most marked characteristic'.[2] He went on to say, ignoring that medieval silver and gold had in his version of a miniature shrine become Victorian granite and lead, that

It is *here* that my original thought of realizing the ideal of the old shrines comes literally into practical operation, for *here* the classes of art and ornamentation displayed in those exquisite works on a scale suggesting only the models of some larger structures are directly reproduced in cognate materials, and to a scale of reality instead of mere miniature models.[3]

Considered as a whole, the mosaics and metalwork on the upper parts of the Albert Memorial were, like the sculptural programme around its base, more ambitious and extensive exercises in their respective media than any comparable rival schemes. It is revealing that while Scott considered these the minor aspects of the Memorial, he also considered them its 'real life and soul',[4] one of the important ways in which its elaborate iconographical programme was demonstrated.

The whole scheme of the upper parts comprises mosaic decorations in the pediments of the gables on each face, idealizing at this height the art – Poetry, Painting, Music, Architecture – of the famous professors lined up in the lapidary Parnassus below, with the spandrels of the arches also carrying mosaic decoration illustrating the practical aspects of that same art;[5] bronze statuary, representative of the sciences (as opposed to art and industry) was set at the angles at two levels, on pedestals of granite against the clustered pillars and in niches above them, while, finally, at the highest level there were statuary representatives of the Christian and moral virtues in the angels and faces of the flèche. At the very top of the Memorial, angels above niches adopted attitudes suggestive of the resignation of worldly honours, followed immediately by another range of more ambitious angels surrounding the base of the cross, whose attitude was intended to be that of aspiration towards heavenly glory.[6] The higher the monument reached, the smaller became the size of its components, but the richer the details, so that the climactic point of the complex allegory of art, industry and Christian life was reached with the globe and the cross which are the Memorial's architectural conclusion.

The mosaic scheme employed on the Albert Memorial was a daring technical (and artistic) experiment: the opportunities for colour the mosaic technique offered were entirely consonant with the popularly increased taste for colour and decoration (although it is surely worth noting that the editors of the Murray *Handbook* of 1872 did not seem to think it

77. General view of the Albert Memorial, showing
the flèche (*Photo: Ben Johnson*).

necessary to illustrate the mosaic decorations). Like most other aspects of the Memorial, the details of the mosaics were late in being fixed; Scott expressing some anxiety during 1864 that neither the contractor nor the type of mosaic had yet been determined.[7] Delay had been incurred by one Minton Campbell who had offered to give one of the mosaics, and this offer ran contrary to Scott's own desired choice of employing Dr Salviati's new, revived Venetian mosaic, which, following some successes with a mosaic portrait of Albert, after Winterhalter, and the decoration of parts of The Albert Memorial Chapel, Windsor, was enjoying something of a vogue,[8] although not before some doubts about the durability of the new medium had been raised. When charged by the Executive Committee that some parts of his Windsor mosaics had deteriorated (Scott believed because of a film caused by 'saline exhalation'[9]), Salviati defended his technique with the bold and imaginative story that this impairment was caused by a misunderstanding in his original brief which had allowed him to believe that the mosaics – which were assembled in his Murano, Venice, workshops – were to be placed high up. Because of this he set the individual stones far apart, a technical device he suggested aided the visual comprehension, thus leaving visible gaps of cement which, when the mosaic was in fact placed nearer eye level, had to be covered with a fresco-type paint which the weather caused to run and spread.[10] Although Salviati's own technique thus sounds a little precarious in its stability, his explanation apparently won him the day, Scott being too cautious to wish to experiment with Minton Campbell's offer of untried mosaic techniques.[11]

Originally, Scott proposed that the subjects illustrated in the gable mosaics should be two historical ones and two allegorical ones: for instance, he gave the installation of Prince Albert as Chancellor of the University of Cambridge and at the Inauguration of the Great Exhibition as examples of the type of subject matter which he would approve.[12] Scott was, however, still undecided about the precise subject matter in September 1864, when he sent sketches of the gables to Eastlake: it may have been the Director of the National Gallery who persuaded Scott to change his design for the gable pediments to personifications of the fine arts, because by June 1865, Scott was saying that he realized the problems of depicting the heroes in modern dress in a timeless memorial and that his taste was turning towards a more ideal and abstract type of representation.[13] Scott was upheld in this idea by John Clayton, of Clayton and Bell, the draughtsman who worked up the designs from the generalized schemes which Scott drew; he too felt that showing the Prince Consort in modern dress in the mosaics, besides clashing with the central statue, would also run the risk of falling into the error of anticlimax[14] (a fault which could be discerned nowhere else on the Memorial).

The final design for the mosaic pediments had them occupied by female allegorical figures, in colour on a gold ground, each representing Poetry, Architecture, Sculpture and Painting, the conceit being to 'resolve the idea which is elaborated in the Podium below'[15]: according to Layard, the 1,100 square feet of exposed mosaic was the largest exterior application of this medium besides the Cathedral of Orvieto.[16] Poetry is on the south front, holding a lyre in her right hand and in her left hand a scroll, with the names of Homer, Virgil, Dante, Shakespeare and Molière inscribed. In the niches of her throne are to be found figures of King David and Homer, while in the spandrels are the figures of the idealized poet and musician. Painting is to the east: she holds a palette and brush, her right hand resting on a stretched canvas: in the niches of her throne are Apelles and Raphael, and the spandrels have idealized figures of a painter with his model. To the north is

78. Clayton and Bell, Poetry, mosaic (*Photo: Ben Johnson*).

79. Clayton and Bell, Architecture, mosaic
(*Photo: Ben Johnson*).

80. Clayton and Bell, Sculpture, mosaic (*Photo: Ben Johnson*).

SCULPTURA

FOR A LIFE DEVOTED TO THE PUBLIC GOOD

81. Clayton and Bell, Painting, mosaic (*Photo: Ben Johnson*).

Architecture, holding a pair of compasses, and a sketch of the Memorial itself, the niches of the throne having Ictinos and Solomon, the one holding a model of the Parthenon, the other a model of the Jewish Temple; in the spandrels appear idealized images of the designer and the builder. The major part of the mosaic scheme was completed by the west side where a female allegorical figure representing sculpture holds a small model in one hand, and a sculptor's mallet in the other. In the niches of her throne are figures of Phidias and Michelangelo, and the spandrels contain, once again, idealized figures of the modeller and the carver.

In executing these mosaics (Plates 78-81), John Clayton caused considerable delay and much official anger by being very dilatory: his full-size oil cartoon technique was considered especially wasteful of time.[17] When accused of these frequent, and some said, deliberate, delays, Clayton said first of all that he needed a bigger studio (at least, that was what Scott believed) and, that excuse being denied him, passed the blame on to the unfortunate Dr Salviati:

In respect of Dr Salviati's demands – which have been in constant urgency under some great pressure of his private affairs, I have, despite all friendly good will and effort in his favour, often found it impossible to keep pace with his convenience.[18]

The precise character of Dr Salviati's private affairs remains obscure, but the effect of his technique is clearly not in doubt. Layard found the general effect of the mosaics when complete, 'rich and harmonious',[19] also praising Clayton for his skill in adapting his designs to the constraints of the medium.

A less ambitious, but only a little less taxing, use of the new mosaics was made in the dedicatory inscription (Plate 82) and in the vault of the canopy (Plates 83-6): the latter was straightforward; against a blue mosaic ground are represented the armorial bearings of the Prince, an inclusion made at Scott's suggestion.[20] The inscription, however, because of the unfamiliar constraints of metre and space – to say nothing of the question of whether Latin or English would be more appropriate – the quatrain formula imposed by the four sides of the Memorial and the final and obvious demand that the whole should, after all, make sense, raised more problems.

Showing little conviction of the timelessness of contemporary English, the Duke of Wellington sought support for a Latin inscription, while both Scott and Layard (in their way, committed modernists), favoured English.[21] The Executive Committee eventually decided to leave the decision to Scott alone, who had already experimented with various different formulae.[22] Scott had first to consider the Queen's suggestion, a rather lacklustre quatrain running 'The Queen and Her People/ To the Memory of Albert Prince Consort/ Born at Coburg August 26 1819/Died at Windsor December 14 1861,'[23] which he essayed in a simple Lombardic letter, one foot, two inches tall, but it was Doyne Bell, to the relief of Scott and the acclamation of the Queen, who came up with the final form of the inscription which Scott had executed in letters of blue glass mosaic with black edges, against a ground of gold enamelled glass: 'Queen Victoria And Her People/To the Memory of Albert Prince Consort/As a Tribute to their Gratitude/For a Life devoted to the Public Good'.[24]

Above this level there are eight bronze statues, in two registers, at the angles. These represent the prominent sciences, at least as they were understood in the mid-nineteenth century: astronomy, chemistry, geology and geometry (on pedestals in front of the clustered columns), rhetoric, medicine, philosophy and physiology (in niches above them). The first

THE:QVEEN:AND:PEOPLE ✤ OF:A:GRATEFVL:NATION

TO:THE:GREAT:AND ✤ ILLVSTRIOUS:PRINCE

WHO:CHOOSING:WISDOM ✤ AS:GOD'S:NOBLEST:GIFT

DEVOTED:IT:SOLELY ✤ TO:THE:PUBLIC:GOOD

82. George Gilbert Scott, inscription sketch (*HM The Queen*).

83. The mosaic vault of the Albert Memorial, photograph taken during construction (*HM The Queen*).

84. George Gilbert Scott, vault sketch (*HM The Queen*).

85 & 86. George Gilbert Scott, vault sketch details (*HM The Queen*).

It would have to be some-
what short, and divided
into four parts each
of which would be divided
into two parts,

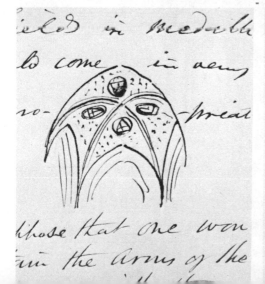

Each of the four principal
lines (on the four fronts)
being divided by a medallion
in its centre.

I presume it would be in
Latin.

On the vaulted ceiling
I have thought that four
shields in medallions
would come   in very
appro-   priately

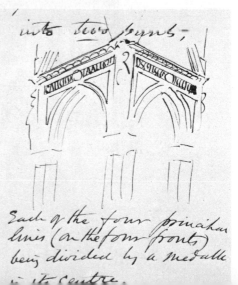

I suppose that one would
contain the Arms of the Prince
impaled with those of
the Queen and the others
contain special armorial
shields of the Prince but

87. View of the Albert Memorial showing H. H. Armstead's and J. B. Philip's bronze statues of the Sciences (*Photo: Jim Styles*).

127

four sciences are represented by figures eight feet, four inches tall, the upper by four figures seven feet, six inches tall.[25] At each level, against the clustered columns and above in the niches, the work of sculpting these figures was shared by H. H. Armstead and J. B. Philip (Plate 87).

Astronomy, which Armstead exhibited independently at the Royal Academy in 1868,[26] is at the south-east angle: a fillet of stars surrounds the figure's head, and she is holding a globe emblematic of the scope of Astronomy and suggestive of the sphere given to Urania by classical sculptors.[27] Armstead also did the figure of Chemistry at the north-east angle, a retort being the emblematic device employed as the emblem of the science, which *The Pall Mall Gazette* found 'simple and vigorous looking . . . there is in the whole design a frank hardihood and a scorn of prettiness'.[28]

The two complementary pieces executed by Philip at the same level as Armstead's Astronomy and Chemistry, were the sciences of Geology and Geometry. His treatment of the figures can be distinguished from Armstead's by a freer and less frontal treatment than Armstead's: they appear to be less likely to have been conceived as a block. Geology, at the north-west angle, has a hammer or a pick-axe in her right hand and a partly exhausted globe in her left, illustrative of the depredations which the search for precious minerals was to make on the earth's surface; at her feet, the same metallic ores and 'antidiluvian remains' characterize further the business of the Geologist.[29] Philip's figure of Geometry is at the south-west angle: she holds a pair of compasses, with her left hand on a tablet inscribed with geometrical lines.[30]

Above this level, where art, industry and the sciences no longer hold sway, the sculpture dwells in the realms of religion and morality. Faith, Hope, Charity and Humility, the prominent Christian virtues, are in the niches

of the spire, with the prominent moral virtues, Fortitude, Justice, Prudence and Temperance, in the angles between them.[31] All were designed by J. Redfern, a sculptor who died in poverty, and executed by the famous metal-working firm, Skidmore of Coventry. Redfern's work (Plates 88-91), effectively invisible from the ground to all but the most acutely perceptive observer, contains some perhaps over-explicit motifs: Hope looks heavenwards, Charity uncovers her bosom and Temperance holds a bridle. Perhaps these figures were admired as little as Redfern's figure of Fortitude, which *The Pall Mall Gazette* said displayed 'with painful evidence that the statuary decorating that work [that is, the Memorial itself] will not all be of a kind to deserve even such measure of praise as we have been able to accord the work of Mr Bell', whose efforts the *Gazette* in turn dismissed as merely clever, while lacking in the more admirable qualities of beauty and nobility.[32]

The most amusingly paradoxical aspect of the art versus the construction of the Albert Memorial is that, considering it was Scott's intention to have created a fairy structure, the means of attaining this whimsical conceit was to employ a considerable amount of heavy engineering. Perhaps that is always the case with fairy structures.

Not all on the Albert Memorial is everything it at first appears, and this remark is not intended to refer to the difficulties experienced in reading some of the sculptures. The main corner columns (which carry capitals (Plate 94) carved by Farmer of Farmer and Brindley, the model-makers, based on French and German examples and the east part of Canterbury Cathedral) are, for instance, a visual deceit, at least in structural terms: the columns and their shafts do not rely on the bronze bands (which appear to bind them) for mutual support: the greater shaft in each columnar group is dovetailed into the central core and sealed with

88 & 89. J. Redfern, bronze statues of Christian and moral virtues in the flèche (*Courtauld Institute of Art*).

90 & 91. J. Redfern, bronze statues of Christian and
moral virtues in the flèche (*Courtauld Institute of
Art*).

131

cement.[33] For greater structural strength, the shafts were jointed at about one-third of their length from the base, while the core was jointed at about the same distance from the capital, thus giving a sturdy overlap: copper cramps and dowels maintained a static performance every bit as good as if the multiple columns were in fact monoliths.[34]

The columns do not entirely support the 210 tons of the flèche, but its weight is taken by a giant diagonal, cruciform box girder, resting on the angles of the structure (Plate 93). It weighs twenty-one tons and is capable of withstanding the thrust of 360 tons.[35] The flèche itself, a masterwork of decorative metalwork and a potent reminder of past beauties, was also a considerable piece of modern engineering.[36] It consists of structural members of cast iron, bolted together and attached to the gable by wrought iron members. This skeleton is covered with ornamental lead, copper and bronze, and on this virgin base it was Skidmore's task to create monumental metal work in which colour must dominate, but which had all the time to be exposed to the weather (Plate 95). The lead covering is nowhere less than a quarter of an inch thick and, besides the surface design which it carries, also acts as a base for innumerable pieces of polished agate, onyx, jasper, cornelian, crystal, marble and granite. On completion, gilding was added.[37]

The flèche rises through a number of different sections, beginning square and becoming first virtually, then entirely, columnar, supporting at its apex the globe and the cross. In its lower stages the lead of the flèche is covered with diaper work, relying on the repeated motif of an alternating 'A' with the crest of the Prince. The next stage, acting as a pedestal to the groups of sculpture, is embossed, and the tabernacles (based on the retablum of Edward I in Westminster Abbey)[38] which house the representations of the Christian and moral virtues are the principal stage of the flèche and

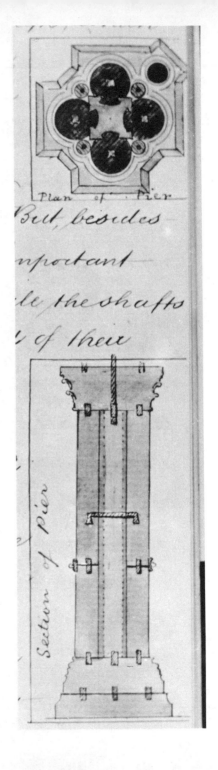

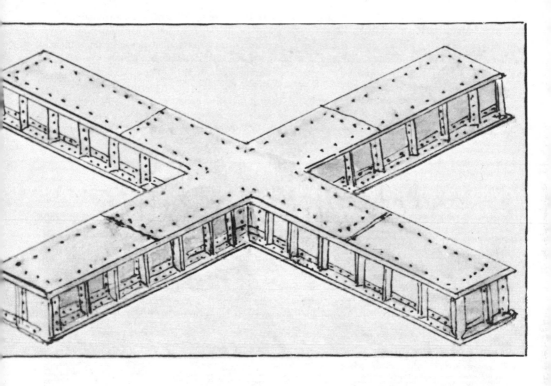

92. George Gilbert Scott, drawing of cross-section of angle column (*HM The Queen*).

93. George Gilbert Scott, drawing of fabricated box-member (*HM The Queen*).

provide in their own formation a reflection of the form of the Memorial itself. The niches are supported by clustered pillars, whose shafts are further enriched with embossing and inlay; their capitals have foliage in copper. So scrupulous was the attention to detail that even the backs of the niches – which could reasonably be left plain – are decorated with rich pattern work: 'parts are not to be neglected because partially concealed',[39] Scott said, although it may be added that, with the contemporary attitude to materials and structure, parts which are wholly concealed may be entirely ignored: beneath the steps of the Memorial there are 396 piers and 868 invisible arches quietly doing their job of sustaining the immense weight of Scott's fairy structure whose decorative possibilities are entirely ignored.[40]

94. Farmer and Brindley, carved capital, photograph taken during construction (*HM The Queen*).

95. Skidmore and Co., decorative metalwork, photograph taken during construction (*HM The Queen*).

96 & 97. Architectural carving in the canopy: details, photographs taken during construction (*HM The Queen*).

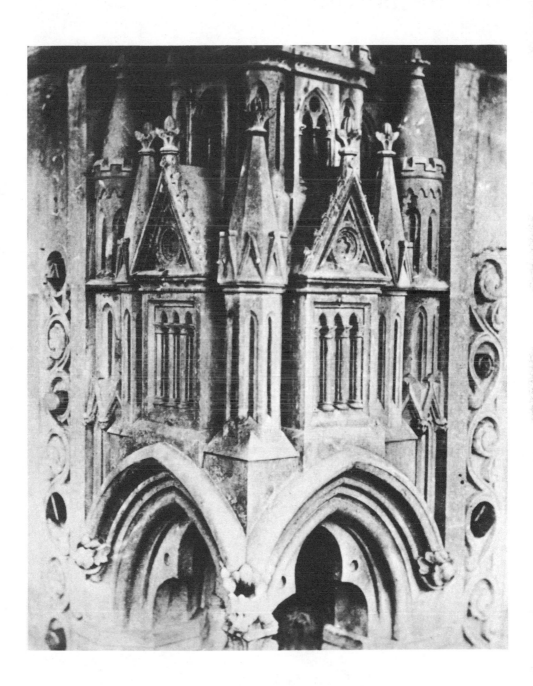

10 Flowers, Fashion and Sunshine

So, on a picturesque labyrinth of arches (itself resting on a bed of concrete nowhere less than seventeen feet thick)[1] a fairy structure falteringly rose. By the mid-1860s, as one correspondent to *The Builder* had cause to remark, Scott's magnificent confection had transformed a part of Hyde Park, once a howling wilderness (used only by such residents of Knightbridge barracks who liked solitude), into a scented arena of 'flowers, fashion and sunshine'.[2] Although the Memorial was at this point chiefly discernible from the distance as a pile of scaffolding standing proud of the surrounding trees, by the agency of his architectural vision Scott had achieved one of the most startling geographical transformations in the history of taste.

A structure as complex as the Albert Memorial could not, of course, be completed quickly and in the monthly reports demanded of Scott by the Queen since July 1864,[3] the energetic and troubled architect provides an eloquent account of the trials which confront him who would create monuments: the reports are a continuous stream of optimism, frustration and despair, diplomatically mixed. For instance, in July 1864 the 'concrete foundations . . . [are] . . . very close upon completion';[4] by December of that year the brick work had been completed, but there were supply difficulties with the troublesome granite;[5] bad weather caused delays in January 1865, but by then the granite had at last arrived and the machinery for polishing the marble was complete and on site, encouraging Scott to note that 'I hope we may now soon see portions of the external work in progress'.[6] In the next month the usually diligent Scott did not submit a Report because of the death of his third son, Albert Henry.[7] By December 1865, after repeated difficulties with the supply of granite, the first visible portions of the Memorial were appearing above the trees.[8]

Continuing problems with the supply of material and the dilatory behaviour of the sculptors delayed progress throughout the later half of the 1860s, putting completion of the Memorial considerably behind schedule and bringing Scott to a state of nervous desperation for which only his limitless energy and enthusiasm could compensate: in a *Retrospective Report* of 1869 the architect explained to the Queen why Armstead's and Philip's sheds still surrounded the base of the Memorial. He says that

. . . scarcely any idea can as yet be formed of its effect when exposed to full view; much less when architectural form becomes clothed with sculpture and is made to harmonize with the rich mosaic work by the free use of Gold and by inlaying of enamel and polished stones,[9]

continuing in a later document that

. . . I can only now add the expression of an earnest hope, that, when the grateful though arduous task is completed, the result may be found in some degree to realize the aspirations with which it was undertaken.[10]

A couple of years earlier, after the elation of solving all the problems with the granite, Scott had organized a dinner for the workmen, to emphasize their *esprit de corps* which he, in a romantic, medievalizing fashion, considered to be a motivating force behind the Memorial. Scott mentions the dinner in his autobiography, but the event was also recorded by R. Coad, Scott's Clerk of Works, in a letter to Doyne Bell of April 1867.[11] Two large tables were improvised out of scaffolding and covered with white paper, and a dinner was prepared for eighty men. Eighty pounds of beef and mutton, sufficient bread, vegetables and cheese were supplied. There were three pints of beer for each man who wanted it, and a curious substance called, rather than described as, 'effervescing' was served to the teetotallers. There was also a dessert of oranges, raisins and nuts. Toasts were offered, in turn, to the Queen, to the architect and to the contractor, while one man was heard to remark how, on

98. Quarrying at Castlewellan, contemporary
photograph (*HM The Queen*).

this pious task, there was a singular lack of profanation among the men.

As the Memorial approached completion, new controversies emerged to replace old ones. A correspondent, pseudonymously 'Epsilon' (who can confidently be identified with the sculptor, John Bell), wrote to the editor of the *Journal of the Royal Society of Arts*, agitating about the site of the Memorial being too remote (an issue long since superseded by events) and the need to have the statue of Albert facing eastwards, to Westminster rather than southwards towards the Horticultural Gardens, and simultaneously suggesting that Foley's seated Prince Albert be replaced by a more devout image of the Prince as a Christian knight, kneeling in prayer (a design for which 'Epsilon's' *alter ego*, John Bell, conveniently had prepared).[12]

Besides this private assault on the Memorial, there was also a degree of Press and Parliamentary comment about aspects of it as it approached completion. This comment was mostly antagonistic to the proposed modifications to the neighbourhood, suggested in the *Kensington Road Improvement Bill*, which was debated in Parliament during May 1870, Lord Elcho objecting to the destruction of forty trees,[13] while an anonymous correspondent in *The Standard* wrote that:

It is earnestly to be hoped that the retired character of Kensington Gardens will not be permitted to be intruded upon. No intellectual man of taste, nor anyone embued with either a feeling of poetry or art, would entertain for a moment the idea of giving an inlet for the rush and roar of London traffic into the exquisite quietude of this beautiful and secluded place . . .[14]

The Times, referring to the unpopular proposal to straighten Kensington Road where it passed the Memorial, mocked the Executive Committee for choosing to build a Memorial 'askew of the road which had always been there'.[15] Taking up the same point, more

moralistically, *The Daily News* reported that 'The public would be far more proud of South Kensington if the very name had not become a synonym for jobbery and intrigue.'[16]

However, a great deal of the virulent criticism was, in fact, generated not so much by the Memorial (which was only its butt), as by the Albert Hall, then taking shape as an adventure entirely independent of the Memorial. Much of the criticism directed at the Memorial was concealed criticism of the jointstock Albert Hall now emerging to fill the gap in Kensington's townscape which had remained since the original proposal to found a Hall of Arts and Sciences in conjunction with the Memorial had been abandoned on account of cost. Some idea of the contemporary reputation of the Hall may be had from a reading of its various nicknames: the New Colosseum, the West End Alhambra, Kensington Circus and, most egregiously, the Cole Hole.[17]

The responsibility for straightening Kensington Road, as well as implicitly defending the very idea of the Memorial, fell to Ayrton, who had taken over from Layard as First Commissioner of Works. Ayrton was not liked. *The Saturday Review* remarked:

We confess that we have under-rated Mr Ayrton's genius for making himself disagreeable. We have long appreciated, and we hope done justice to his capacity for inventing and perfecting annoyances in the discharge of his official duty,[18]

and the same writer demanded to know whether the artistic, practical or financial evils of the *Improvement Bill* were the most glaringly in error. *The Daily Telegraph* said that Ayrton, in his advocacy of the re-siting of the Kensington Road, showed 'a contempt for popularity which is little less than heroic'.[19] Not surprisingly, with so much opinion against it, the *Kensington Road Improvement Bill* was defeated in Parliament, 'with general cheering from every part of the House',[20] giving the Liberal

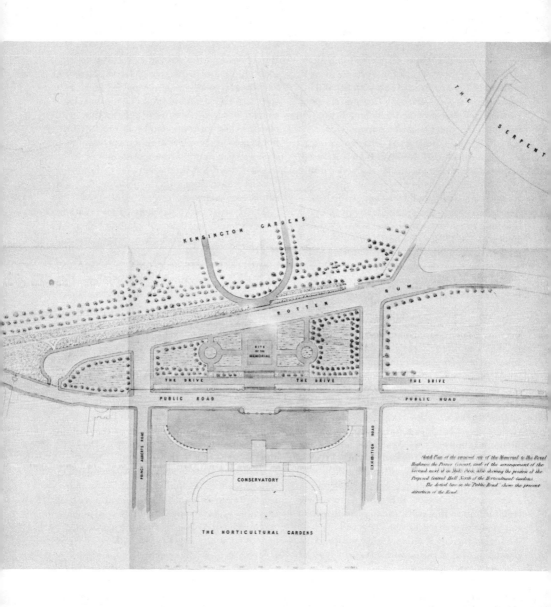

99. Proposed site of the Albert Memorial (*HM The Queen*).

government its first defeat of consequence since elevation to office. However, this was no more than a temporary setback for Ayrton's plans and intentions: he went ahead with the Bill in making it a *de facto* necessity to widen the road by the ingenious method of blocking Rotten Row (a policy of which the Queen apparently approved)[21] and causing congestion of traffic. By this means he had his way. Widely accused of despotism and of absurdity, Ayrton skilfully orchestrated the whole business of improving Kensington Road, and it was largely by his efforts that workmen were able to put the finishing touches to the Memorial's steps during February 1871,[22] leaving only sourpuss antagonists, such as the anonymous corres-pondent who wrote to the Albert Hall, claiming that the Memorial was unstable,[23] to cavil about invented problems, anxieties and expenses. It seems again that the disappointed and bitter – not to say wayward – John Bell, the sculptor, may have been the author of this letter,[24] at least according to Scott, who considered this mischievous structural criticism merely to be the latest development in John Bell's hectoringly advanced arguments that the Memorial needed a central support to remain stable.[25]

Despite the varieties of adverse comment in the Press, in Parliament and in private, the Memorial showed every sign of becoming a great popular success: as early as July 1870[26] arrangements were being made for police protection, and the First Commissioner was empowered to close the gates of the protective iron railings so that no 'idle and disordly persons' might sleep or lie within the Consort's commemorative precincts. Public meetings, preaching and lecturing were also forbidden in the area of the enclosure.[27]

By 23 April 1872, Scott could write to Doyne Bell, saying that his own part in the creation of the Memorial was drawing to a close,[28] his sole remaining official duty being to be there, at the Memorial, when the Queen arrived for an official inspection at the beginning of July. Her Majesty caught the train from Windsor to Paddington and drove straight to the Memorial. She found it 'really magnificent',[29] admiring specially Theed's Africa and Foley's Asia. Of course, 'dearest Albert's statue'[30] was not in place at the time (nor would it be until 1875), but it is clear from Her Majesty's private *Journals* that a public inauguration was envisaged for that time when Foley's bronze consort was hoisted atop the podium in the now sunny Kensington.

The delays of art overwhelmed royal patience, however, and long before the failing Foley (who died in 1874) could finish the central statue of the Prince, the Memorial was informally opened to the public early in August 1872, after the Press and Private views which followed the Queen's inspection.[31] It was only at this time that Armstead's and Philip's lean-to sheds were removed and their lapidary Parnassus which surrounds the base of the Memorial revealed to the general public. . . . And popular approval was hyperbolic: Colonel Henderson of the Metropolitan Police cautiously reported on the 'general admiration'[32] aroused by the monument as well as the impressive number of citizens who visited the site. According to Doyne Bell, less happily. The policemen on duty at the podium have been several times overcome by the heat, glare and the breath of the crowd . . .'[33]

More than three years later, when Foley's central statue was finally put in place (and by which time public enthusiasm might have been expected to have waned), there was so much commotion and clamour that the workmen employed on the job of raising Albert were not able to erect his effigy because of the crush.[34]

By this time Scott was nearing the end of his own career, and the contractor, Kelk, was already retired. The Queen suggested that honours might be appropriate.[35] Gladstone first of all wrote to Scott, offering him a knighthood,[36] and only reluctantly (because of

100. Kensington Road before the alteration plan
(*HM The Queen*).

101. Kensington Road after the alteration plan
(*HM The Queen*).

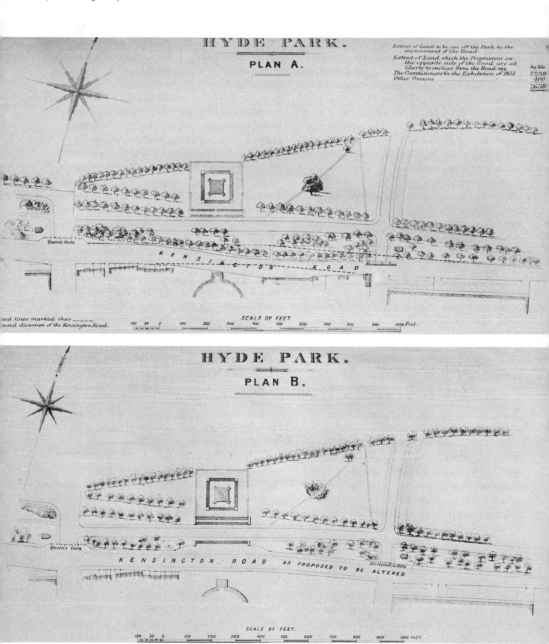

a clash of political opinions) extending the same honour to Kelk a couple of days later.[37] Amid justified rumours that he expected a superior honour from a future government more close to his own political views, the contractor declined his knighthood.[38] Gladstone no doubt felt relieved in private, but commented on the record that as no painter, sculptor or architect since Godfrey Kneller had been made a baronet, then it would be invidious to raise Kelk to the baronetcy above Scott.[39]

What did informed opinion make of Scott's achievement? *The Architectural Journal* declared, rather cattily, that 'The superstructure certainly seems more in the style of that art which gave birth to the Lord Mayor's state carriage than anything else,'[40] a peculiarly happy comment, if it is recalled what the Lord Mayor's original role was in creating the Memorial. In fact, despite a generalized popular approval of this largest mass of modern sculpture (if the excitable contemporary Press reports can be relied on),[41] the professional attitude to the Albert Memorial was not always so enthusiastic. At the same time the emphatic monument to patriotism, to piety and to art has not ridden the peaks and the troughs of historiography with facility. As chief symbol of the Gothic Revival in Britain it has suffered the same critical traumas as the movement itself: in his pioneering article on Scott, Martin Shaw Briggs, author of *The Architect in History*, did not even bother to illustrate the Memorial,[42] and Rupert Gunnis refers to an un-named source, spiritually close to General Grey, who described it as ' . . . a confection of gingerbread which ought to be under a glass shade on a giant's mantel-piece.'[43]

In 1979, with the Memorial's status as a landmark assured, but its position in the history of nineteenth-century art perhaps not yet satisfactorily defined, an American tourist was overheard to say that 'it has all the earmarks of an eyesore'.[44] To Charles Handley-Read the

Memorial was a 'test for taste',[45] and Stephen Potter made the most amusing use of its metaphorical potential in describing Professor Saintsbury as an 'Albert Memorial of learning'.[46] Hermione Gingold wished to take it with her to her BBC Desert Island, along with her discs,[47] while, perhaps more pertinent, Viollet-le-Duc – Europe's most distinguished theoretical exponent of the Gothic Revival – found Scott's design typical of much that he found wanting in contemporary English architecture: qualities like unity and harmony, for instance, while he deplored Scott's elaborate sham in the constructional technique, citing as superior examples of architecture, the functional tradition of English schools, hospitals, railway stations and factories.[48] Following a line of thought similarly dependant on structural utilitarianism for critical values, a contemporary correspondent in *The Builder* criticized Scott for disguising his means of construction, by laying gingerbread over box girders.[49]

Edmund Gosse, perhaps considering sculpture in front of architecture, found it a 'very striking monument, full of talent, full of force'.[50] Sir William Conway agreed: the biographer of Dürer thought that Scott had created 'beyond question the finest monumental structure in Europe'.[51] Lytton Strachey, writing at a time when the Gothic Revival as a whole was awaiting Kenneth Clark's canonical essay in the history of taste, was amused by Scott's monument.[52] R.G. Collingwood was less moved to favour it. The philosopher was shocked by its extravagance. A sequence of strolls through the Park allowed Collingwood to accumulate the opinion that the monument was 'visibly mis-shapen, corrupt, crawling, verminous'[53] although it should be added that, despite this criticism, the general effect of Scott's design was powerful enough to move him to produce a study, called *Truth and Contradiction*, which attempted to deal with the perplexing problems, perceptual and ideological, which the jarring Memorial caused him. It was never published.

The architect did not live for long after the Albert Memorial's completion.[54] He had realized an imaginary structure out of precious materials and translated a desolate area of London park into a celebrated focus of high art. Of course, the Albert Memorial can appear absurd: in a utilitarian age it seems gross, in a gross age it may seem inarticulate. And it cost the architect dearly, even though it won him a knighthood. He had often remarked himself that this particular monumental idea was so new as to arouse much opposition. The bureaucracy wearied Scott. In his posthumously published autobiography, he admitted of the future of the Memorial: 'I as yet have no idea how it may end.'[55] It might be recalled, therefore, that at the very beginning, Sir Charles Beaumont Phipps had mentioned to his colleague, General Grey, that the Albert Memorial 'will be the architectural work of the time to which most attention in this country will be called'.[56] Of course, this was accurately prophetic, and the answer to Scott's question is to be found . . . here.

Notes

Prologue

1. The most comprehensive life of Prince Albert is that of Theodore Martin, the official biographer, who began his monumental work as a memorandum and ended up spending almost twelve years of his life on it; it is published as *The Life of HRH The Prince Consort*, 5 vols, 1875–80.

    Martin also wrote the entry on the Prince in *The Dictionary of National Biography* (referred to hereafter as *DNB*), vol. I, pp. 217–31. After the Prince's death there were many laudatory obituaries, of which the one appearing in *Blackwood's Magazine*, vol. 91, January 1862, pp. 131–5 is typical. Two recent studies of the Prince Consort's life are Winslow Ames, *Prince Albert and Victorian Taste*, Chapman and Hall, 1967, and David Duff, *Albert and Victoria*, Muller, 1972. The most recent biography of the Prince Consort is Daphne Bennett's *King without a Crown*, Heinemann, 1977.

    Prince Albert regarded his own greatest achievement as the Great Exhibition of 1851, when all the world's industries were brought together in Hyde Park. When faced, in 1860, with a proposal from the ambitious mayor that a memorial should be erected even before his death, the Prince was nonplussed. He described his feelings in a letter to the Earl of Granville: ' . . . the people have a perfect right to . . . erect a monument in remembrance of the Great Exhibition – nor could I volunteer to say "you must not connect it in any way with me." ' (Royal Archives [referred to hereafter as RA] F25/183.)

    However, eschewing humbug, as he put it, Prince Albert maintained that he did not want his own likeness to form any part of a proposed memorial: ' . . . as it would both disturb my quiet rides in Rotten Row to see my own face staring at me: & if (as is very likely), it became an artistic monstrosity, like most of our monuments, it wd. upset my equanimity to be permanently ridiculed and laughed at in effigies . . . ' (RA F25/183.)

2. *DNB*, p. 221.
3. George Gilbert Scott, *Personal and Professional Recollections*, p. 92; *The Builder*, vol. I, 1843, pp. 458–9.
4. *DNB*, loc. cit.
5. *DNB*, p. 231.
6. *The Times*, 23 January 1862.
7. In his article, 'The Albert Memorial', *Architectural Review*, vol. 135, 1964, p. 423, Peter Ferriday offers a very amusing account of Prince Albert's popular reputation.
8. *The Times*, 16 December 1861.
9. Alfred, Lord Tennyson, line 43, Dedication to *The Idylls of the King*: see Christopher Ricks (ed.) *The Poems of Tennyson*, Longmans, 1969, p. 1468.
10. *The Times*, 23 December 1861, p. 6.
11. A representative collection of press cuttings is preserved in RA Add. H2, pp. 1–1a.

Chapter 1: An Idea for a Monument

1. The *DNB* describes Cole as an 'official'; in fact, he was a leading figure in the administration of the arts in Britain in the middle of the nineteenth century. He began his career at the Record Office in 1838 and rose to serve on the managing committees of the international exhibitions in 1851, 1862 and 1871–4. He was a water-colourist, etcher and engraver, a part-time editor and, as Secretary of the Science and Art Department from 1858 to 1873, may be regarded as the creator of the Victoria and Albert Museum.
2. RA Add. H2/2–3. Henry Cole's open letter was dated 31 December 1861. Cole may have known that the Prince himself had only wished to be memorialized by stones marking the corners of the site of the Great Exhibition, with any surplus left over from a public subscription being given to 'the Erection of the Museums of Art and Science'. RA F25/183.
3. The cutting is preserved in the Royal Archives, Add. H2/21.
4. William Cubitt was Lord Mayor of London and a partner in his brother Thomas's famous building firm, becoming the sole proprietor after 1855. He was MP for Andover from 1847 to 1861 and Lord Mayor from 1860 to 1862. He died in 1863.
5. *The Times*, 14 January 1862.
6. RA Add. H1/1.
7. *Minute Book of the Prince Consort Memorial*, RA Add. H6/1, dated 14 January 1862.
8. This was reported in *The Times*, 15 January 1862.
9. *The Builder*, vol. 21, 4 April 1863, p. 233. By 1863 *The Builder* was becoming critical of the principles instituted at the Mansion House meeting. The paper was concerned about the meeting casting on to the Queen the responsibility for the final appearance of the Albert Memorial. It was felt that Her Majesty's provision of the design would not be beneficial to architecture.
10. On Schinkel's stage designs, see Maurice Raraty, *Hoffmann and his Theatre*, unpublished PhD thesis, University of Sheffield, 1964, pp. 247–57; Hermann Pundt, *Schinkel's Berlin*, Harvard, 1972, fig. 50; W. D. Robson-Scott, *The Literary Background to the Gothic Revival in Germany*, Athlone Press, 1965, p. 233 and Pl. 5.

11. Pundt. op. cit. p. 251, n. 8.
12. Rauch lived from 1777 to 1857. On his life and works see Thieme-Becker, *Allgemeines Lexikon der Bildenden Kunstler*, Band XXVIII, S. 37.
13. RA Add. 1/17A, p. 4.
14. RA Add. H7/127.
15. On Kemp, who was the son of a shepherd and who eventually drowned in the Union Canal, see the life written by his nephew, Thomas Bonnar. More recently W. Forbes Gray, 'The Scott Monument and its Architect', *Architectural Review*, vol. 26, July 1944, pp. 26–7, and Ann Martha Wrinch, 'George Kemp and the Scott Monument', *Country Life*, 5 August 1971, pp. 322–3 are both very useful.
16. John Ruskin, *Fors Clavigera* (*The Works of John Ruskin*, Library Edition, ed. Cook and Wedderburn, London 1903–12), vol. 27, p. 565, letter 31, July 1873.
17. Gray, op. cit.
18. Charles-Auguste Questel, architect, lived from 1807 to 1888; Jean Jacques Pradier, sculptor, lived from 1790 to 1852. The fountain at Nimes which was their chief collaborative work is illustrated on the title-page of *Nîmes*, Collection des Guides-Joannes, Hachette, Paris, 1909, and also in J. Charles-Roux, *Nîmes*, Bloud, Paris, 1908, interleaved between pp. 104–5.
19. Guide-Joannes, op. cit., p. 41.
20. *Recollections*, p. 89.
21. Ibid., pp. 89–90.
22. W. B. Fredeman, *Pre-Raphaelite Journal*, Oxford, 1975, p. 93.
23. Pietro Tenerani, sculptor, lived from 1798 to 1869. A pseudonymous letter published in *The Times*, 15 January 1862, is evidence of popular approval of Tenerani's design.
24. RA Add. H12.
25. Ibid.
26. Ibid.
27. Ferriday, op. cit., p. 424.
28. RA Add. H12.
29. *The Times*, 1 December 1862.
30. RA Add. H12.
31. RA Add. H12, Dedicatory Letter to Her Majesty The Queen.
32. RA Add. H12.
33. Ibid. Besides the preceding examples mentioned in cuttings or memoranda in the Royal Archives, Ferriday (op. cit.) refers to a handful of other monuments, institutional and sculpted, from Wolverhampton to Kennington, which were raised to Prince Albert's memory.
34. *The Builder*, 8 November 1862, p. 805.
35. *Report*, RA Add. H12.
36. *The Builder*, vol. 20, 27 September 1862, p. 699.
37. At the same time, Noble also had designs and a mould for a companion statue to that of Her Majesty, already in Peel Park. His design showed the Prince in the Robes of the Chancellor of Oxford University and was promptly accepted by the Salford Committee responsible for municipal parkland statuary.
38. *The Builder*, 27 September 1862, p. 699, gives: length of steps at base 35 feet; base 19 feet; height to top of vane 75 feet; height of basement $13\frac{1}{2}$ feet; height of pedestal 8 feet 2 inches. The cost was intended to be kept down to £4–5000, but eventually rose to some £6079 9s 3d, RA Add. H12, for work which eventually lasted five years.

Chapter 2: The Competition for the Albert Memorial

1. Cole's letter is actually dated 31 December 1861. RA Add. H2/2–3.
2. Prince Albert's own desire to have an institutional memorial, especially one devoted to 'promoting Science and Arts as applied to productive industry' is recorded in a letter of 23 April 1862 from General Grey to Sir Charles Eastlake. RA Add. H1, 24–6.
3. RA Add. H2/2–3.
4. Lieutenant-General the Hon. Charles Grey spent his life in royal service: an equerry from 1837 to 1867; Private Secretary to Prince Albert from 1849; Joint Keeper of the Privy Purse with Sir Thomas Biddulph from 1866–7; Private Secretary to the Queen from 1867 to his death in 1870. On Grey's death Gilbert Scott wrote to Doyne Bell, expressing his sympathy, but telling us a little about the circumstances of their acquaintance: 'My own relations with him have been but those of a professional man with a client.'
5. Ferriday, op. cit., p. 424, cites one example, for instance.
6. RA Add. H6/1.
7. Ibid.
8. Sir Charles Lock Eastlake studied art under the history painter, Benjamin Robert Haydon, and his early career was spent as a painter, in Paris and Rome. He failed to become Professor of Fine Arts at London University in both 1833 and 1836, but became Secretary of the Fine Art Commission and was a Commissioner of the Great Exhibition of 1851. He became Director of the National Gallery in 1855 and published a translation of Goethe's *Farbenlehre*, a book on *Materials for the History of Oil Painting* and a monumental study of the Gothic Revival. When he died, in 1865, his

place as artistic adviser to the Queen was taken by Layard.

9. RA Add. H12/66.

10. Ibid.

11. John Bell, the sculptor, had contributed a lengthy paper called 'Some Remarks on . . . the Obelisk' in *The Journal of the Royal Society of Arts*, no. 340, vol. VII, 27 May 1859, pp. 475–85. As a letter to Eastlake proves, Scott had been thinking of a gilded and bejewelled Albert Memorial. Eastlake had expressed interest, but said he could do nothing about it. RA Add. H1/290.

12. RA Add. H1/22.

13. RA Add. I/17A p. 4.

14. RA Add. H2/79–80.

15. RA Add. H7/16.

16. RA Add. H6/7.

17. RA Add. H6/11.

18. RA Add. H6/13.

19. RA Add. H1/174.

20. Ibid.

21. RA Add. H1/307–8.

22. F. T. Palgrave, 'New Aspects of the Albert Memorial', *The London Review*, 26 April 1862, pp. 65–6. Later, Palgrave was to gather together all his thoughts on the Albert Memorial and publish them as a critical attack in his *Essays on Art*, Macmillan, 1866, pp. 280–98.

23. RA Add. H1/247–8.

24. Ibid.

25. Nikolaus Pevsner, 'An unknown Albert Memorial', *Architectural Review*, vol. 146, December 1969, p. 469. On Hittorff there is Karl Hammer, *Jakob Ignaz Hittorff, ein Pariser Baumeister*, Pariser Historische Studien, Band VI, Verlag Anton Hiesermann, Stuttgart, 1968.

26. *RIBA Papers*, Session 1866–7, Occasional Papers, 8 April 1867; Gavin Stamp, 'Sir Gilbert Scott's Recollections', *Architectural History*, vol. 19, 1976, pp. 54–73.

27. *Architectural Review*, vol. 15, 1904, p. 193; *The Builder*, vol. 31, 1873, pp. 817–18; *Architectural Review*, vol. 115, 1954, p. 314.

28. Victoria and Albert Museum, Department of Prints and Drawings D. 1094–1886.

29. RA Add. H6/15.

30. RA Add. H1/211.

31. Ibid.

32. RA Add. H6/16.

33. RA Add. H6/17–18. Charles Barry, who was not originally invited to compete, in fact sent in designs with the others selected.

34. RA Add. H1/283.

35. Ibid.

36. RA Add. H1/284.

37. RA Add. H6/18–19.

38. RA Add. H7/57–8.

39. Ibid.

40. RA Add. H7/60.

41. RA Add. H6/22.

42. RA Add. H6/24.

43. RA Add. H7/63.

44. RA Add. H7/79.

45. RA Add. H7/83.

46. RA Add. H1/425.

47. RA Add. H1/423.

48. RA Add. H1/433.

49. RA Add. H7/86.

50. RA Add. H7/86–7.

51. RA Add. H1/431.

52. RA Add. H7/90; RA Add. H1/429.

53. RA Add. H7/96.

54. RA Add. H7/126.

55. Philip Charles Hardwick (1822–92) was the son of Philip Hardwick (1792–1870). The younger man took over the practice after the decline of his father's health in the late 1840s. Howard Colvin, *A Biographical Dictionary of English Architects 1660–1840*, Murray, 1954, pp. 263–4.

56. *The Builder*, 4 April 1863, p. 233.

57. RA Add. H8/2. Hardwick's drawings are in the Drawings Collection of the RIBA at X16/10(1–3).

58. RA Add. H8/4.

59. Donaldson's printed submission, for the Queen's inspection, is RA Add. 1/17a. It is dated 23 January 1863. [The various submissions received from the architects are bound together with Royal Archives at RA Add. H1/17a, and the pages of the separate submissions are not distinguished from one another.] Donaldson's drawings are in the Drawings Collection of the RIBA at X16/6(1–3).

60. RA Add. H1/17a, p. 3.

61. RA Add. H1/17a, p. 4.

62. Ibid.

63. RA Add. H1/17a, p. 6.

64. RA Add. H1/17a, p. 7.

65. The drawings appear to be lost, but Sir James Pennethorne's description of his design is preserved in RA Add. 1/17a.

66. RA Add. H1/17a, p. 8.

67. Ibid.

68. RA Add. H1/17a, p. 12.

69. Eastlake to Pennethorne, 10 May 1862, RA Add. H7/48.

70. The drawings appear to be lost, although

Pennethorne's layout sketch is preserved in PRO *Works* 35/68.

71. RA Add. H1/17a.
72. RA Add. H1/17a, p. 1.
73. RA Add. H1/17a, p. 2.
74. *The Builder*, 4 April 1863, p. 233.
75. RA Add. H1/17a, p. 2.
76. Ibid.
77. RA Add. H1/17a, p. 3.
78. RA Add. H1/17a, p. 4.
79. Ibid.
80. See, for instance, Stephen Bayley, 'A British Schinkel', *Architectural Association Quarterly*, vol. 7, no. 4, April–June, 1975, pp. 28–32.
81. RA Add. H1/17a, p. 8.
82. RA Add. H1/17a, ms. n.p.
83. RA Add. H1/17a, p. 5.
84. Stamp, op cit., 58; RA Add. H1/17a, p. 1.
85. RA Add. H1/17a, p. 3.
86. Ibid.
87. Ibid.
88. RA Add. H1/17a, p. 6.
89. *The Builder*, 4 April 1863, p. 233. The designs by Charles Barry are in the Drawings Collection of the RIBA at X16/10(6–8). *The Catalogue of the Drawings Collection of the RIBA*, Gregg, Farnborough, 1972, mentions only two unidentified designs for a large, porticoed building, p. 48.
90. RA Add. H1/17a, n.p. Some of Scott's drawings of the Memorial are in the Drawings Collection of the RIBA at O812 (1–2); PRO *Works* 35/69 88, 93–101, 108.
91. RA Add. H1/17a, p. 5.
92. RA Add. H1/17a, p. 6.
93. RA Add. H1/17a, p. 7.
94. Ibid.
95. RA Add. H1/17a, p. 8.
96. RA Add. H1/17a, p. 11.
97. RA Add. H1/17a, p. 13.
98. *Illustrated London News*, 11 July 1863, pp. 48–9.
99. *The Builder*, vol. 21, 4 April 1863, p. 233.
100. RA Add. H2/434–42, printed as pp. 3–15.
101. RA Add. H6/37.
102. RA Add. H2/434–42, p. 6.
103. Ibid.
104. RA Add. H2/434–42, p. 7.
105. RA Add. H2/442.
106. RA Add. H2/469.
107. Ibid. In fact, Scott had ultimately to reduce the height of the Albert Memorial from 185 feet to 148 feet, for reasons of economy. RA Add. H6/49.
108. RA Add. H2/626.
109. RA Add. H2/779–80.

110. *The Builder*, vol. 20, 1862, p. 75.

Chapter 3: Scott's Design

1. M. S. Briggs, 'Sir Gilbert Scott, RA', *Architectural Review*, vol. 24, August 1908, pp. 92–100; Sept. 1908, pp. 147–52; Oct. 1908, pp. 180–5; Dec. 1908, pp. 290–5; on Scott's life see *DNB*, vol. XVII, pp. 957–9.
2. *DNB*, vol. XVII, p. 1012.
3. *Recollections*, p. 92: *The Builder*, vol. I, 1843, pp. 458–9.
4. Briggs, op. cit., p. 93; *Recollections*, p. 89.
5. Briggs, op. cit., p. 92.
6. Ibid., p. 96.
7. *DNB*, vol. XVII, p. 958.
8. Briggs, op cit., p. 98.
9. The *Ecclesiologist*, vol. I, new series, no. 4, p. 184.
10. *Recollections*, pp. 135–72.
11. For a fuller description of the Martyrs' Memorial, see Jennifer Sherwood and Nikolaus Pevsner, *Oxfordshire*, The Buildings of England, Penguin, 1974, pp. 313–14.
12. *Recollections*, p. 88. Scott says he was 'exceedingly irate at the projected destruction by Mr Barry of St. Stephen's Chapel', *Recollections*, p. 87, and wrote to Pugin about it. To his 'almost tremulous delight' he was invited to visit, *Recollections*, p. 89.
13. *Recollections*, p. 89.
14. Ibid.
15. RA Add. H2/2867.
16. Briggs, op. cit., p. 152.
17. RA Add. H2/484.
18. Ibid.
19. RA Add. H2/489.
20. The 18 page pamphlet is inserted in RA Add. H2/491–4.
21. RA Add. H2/5
22. Ibid.
23. RA Add. H2/6.
24. RA Add. H4/19.
25. RA Add. H4/3.
26. Ibid.
27. RA Add. H4/4.
28. RA Add. H4/5.
29. Ibid.
30. *The Survey of London*, vol. XXXVIII, *The Museums Area of South Kensington and Westminster*, Athlone Press, 1975, chapter X, pp. 148–76; RA Add. H2/569–70. Captain Francis Fowke also commented on the similarity of the two designs, while on a visit to Italy in 1863, Mangeot Family Papers, ms. account of the tour by Francis Fowke, 1863, p. 190. The drawing is in the Victoria and

Albert Museum, Department of Prints and Drawings, No. 104.

31. *The Times*, 23 April 1863.
32. Ibid.
33. *DNB*, vol. IV, pp. 724–6.
34. Henry Cole ms. *Diaries*, 1863, Victoria and Albert Museum, n.p.
35. Ibid.
36. A proof copy is preserved in RA Add. H2/515. A final copy was printed for private circulation in 1863. RA Add. H2/519–24.
37. Ibid.
38. Charles Beaumont Phipps was born in 1801 and was an equerry to the Queen from 1846 to 1849. He became Keeper of the Privy Purse in October 1849 and retained that appointment until his death in 1866. He had also served as Treasurer and Cofferer to Prince Albert.
39. RA Add. H2/571.
40. On Scott and the Foreign Office business, see Peter Ferriday, *Victorian Architecture*, Cape, 1963, pp. 96–7; *Recollections*, p. 266.
41. RA Add. H2/544; this was the covering note which Phipps sent to Grey with Cole's and Scott's notes, 9 May 1863.
42. RA Add. H2/545.
43. RA Add. H2/547–9.
44. Ibid.
45. Ibid.
46. RA Add. H2/548.
47. RA Add. H2/500.
48. RA Add. H2/551.
49. RA Add. H2/558.
50. Ibid.
51. RA Add. H2/561.
52. RA Add. H2/564.
53. RA Add. H2/565.
54. RA Add. H2/562.
55. Ibid.
56. RA Add. H4/7.
57. RA Add. H4/19–20.
58. The model passed into the South Kensington Museum of Construction. It is now in the Victoria and Albert Museum, no. 41 a. Y. See John Physick and Michael Darby, *Marble Halls*, Victoria and Albert Museum, 1973, pp. 213–14.
59. John Kelk made a fortune, principally with railway contracting (he built Victoria station), but his firm also erected the 1862 exhibition and the Alexandra Palace. Millais painted his portrait in 1870. It was during work on the 1862 exhibition that Kelk met Henry Cole. Kelk made an offer, whether directly stimulated by Cole we do not

know, to erect the Memorial at cost price. Scott suspected his motives and was anxious lest the power invested in Cole by a parsimonious administration would undermine his own.
60. RA Add. H2/763.

Chapter 4: Continents, Skills and Parnassus

1. *Recollections*, p. 177f.
2. Ibid., p. 266.
3. RA Add. H2/800–1.
4. *The Builder*, vol. 21, 23 May 1863.
5. James Fergusson, *A History of Architecture in All Countries*, was published, for instance, in 2 vols. 1865–7; C. R. Cockerell's *Iconography of the West Front of Wells Cathedral* in 1851.
6. RA Add. H2/800.
7. *Recollections*, p. 266.
8. RA Add. H2/799.
9. Ibid.
10. Ibid.
11. RA Add. H2/741–2.
12. RA Add. H2/743.
13. RA Add. H2/746.
14. RA Add. H2/755.
15. RA Add. H2/798.
16. Ibid.
17. RA Add. H2/798.
18. RA Add. H2/798–9.
19. RA Add. H2/799.
20. RA Add. H2/798.
21. Ibid.
22. RA Add. H2/785.
23. Ibid.
24. RA Add. H2/811.
25. Ibid.
26. Ibid.
27. RA Add. H2/818.
28. RA Add. H2/826.
29. RA Add. H2/829.
30. RA Add. H2/3949.

Chapter 5: The Unstained Princely Gentleman

1. RA Add. H2/817.
2. RA Add. H2/861.
3. RA Add. H2/865.
4. RA Add. H2/867.
5. RA Add. H2/866, 1724.
6. RA Add. H2/867.
7. Fanny Aikin-Kortright, *The Court Suburb Magazine*, No. 10, July 1869, pp. 429–31.
8. RA Add. H2/1302.
9. RA Add. H2/1302, 1306.
10. RA Add. H2/1307.

11. RA Add. H2/1309, 1317.
12. RA Add. H2/1316.
13. RA Add. H2/1321–2.
14. RA Add. H2/2019. Sir Austin Henry Layard was an archaeologist (who excavated Nineveh) and politician (Liberal MP for Aylesbury, 1852–7). Layard advised the Queen on artistic matters after Eastlake's death and became Chief Commissioner of Works from 1868 to 1869. Layard spent the years 1869 to 1877 at the Madrid Embassy during which time Sir Charles Newton, Keeper of Greek and Roman Antiquities at the British Museum, continued to advise the Queen on aesthetic matters.
15. RA Add. H2/2020.
16. RA Add. H2/2021, 2024.
17. RA Add. H2/1826–7.
18. RA Add. H2/2035–6.
19. Ibid.
20. RA Add. H2/2049.
21. RA Add. H2/2043.
22. RA Add. H2/2054.
23. RA Add. H2/2056; to see how impressive on a sensitive artist was the necessity of a seated Albert statue, it is interesting to note that H. H. Armstead privately prepared designs for a sitting Prince Consort (Royal Academy, H. H. Armstead, Red scrapbook, n.p., n.d.).
24. *The Daily Telegraph*, 8 July 1867.
25. RA Add. H2/2064.
26. RA Add. H2/2066.
27. RA Add. H2/2080.
28. RA Add. H2/2075.
29. RA Add. H2/2077.
30. RA Add. H2/2078.
31. Ibid.
32. RA Add. H2/2442.
33. *The Kensington News*, 6 August 1870.
34. RA Add. H2/2461.
35. RA Add. H2/2436.
36. RA Add. H2/2462.
37. RA Add. H2/2498.
38. RA Add. H2/2378.
39. RA Add. H2/2393.
40. RA Add. H2/2393, 2398–9.
41. RA Add. H2/2400.
42. RA Add. H11.
43. Ibid.
44. RA Add. H2/2779.
45. RA Add. H2/2924.
46. RA Add. H2/2926.
47. RA Add. H2/2966.
48. RA Add. H2/3094.
49. RA Add. H2/3263.
50. RA Add. H2/3340.
51. RA Add. H2/3361.
52. RA Add. H2/3726.
53. RA Add. H2/3524.
54. Ibid.
55. Doyne Bell worked in the Privy Purse from 1853, when he started filing expenses claims, and became Secretary to the Privy Purse in 1867. He died in 1888.
56. RA Add. H2/4305.
57. RA Add. H2/4318.
58. RA Add. H2/4451.
59. RA Add. H2/4440.
60. RA Add. H2/2515.
61. RA Add. H2/4542.
62. RA Add. H2/4586–7.
63. *The Daily News*, 11 March 1876; although more favourable reports appeared in *The Times*, 13 March 1876, *The Morning Post*, 13 March 1876, and *The Illustrated London News*, 18 March 1876.

Chapter 6: Parnassus

1. Sir Charles Eastlake, *Contributions to the Literature of Fine Arts*, Murray, 1848, pp. 29–50.
2. Norman D. Ziff, *Paul Delaroche – A Study in C19th French History Painting*, Garland, New York, 1977, p. 176, n.25.
3. cf. Ziff, op. cit., p. 182. Delaroche's painting was widely known in England; certainly Daniel Maclise knew and admired it and it was the subject of a modest study by Mrs Jameson, *A Description and Analysis of the Great Picture by Paul Delaroche on the Semicircular Wall of the Amphitheatre of the School of Fine Arts at Paris*, London, n.d.
4. RA Add. H4/31.
5. RA Add. H4/10.
6. Ibid.
7. RA Add. H4/11.
8. RA Add. H2/821.
9. Ibid.
10. *Handbook to the Prince Consort National Memorial*, Murray, 1872, pp. 32–3.
11. RA Add. H2/945.
12. RA Add. H2/954.
13. *Handbook*, p. 33.
14. On this aspect see Francis Haskell, *Rediscoveries in Art*, Oxford, 1976, pp. 9–23.
15. RA Add. H2/1592–6; *Handbook*, pp. 36, 46. The complete complements of Poets and Musicians is: Auber, Mehul, Rameau, Lulli (sic), Grétry, Josquin des Prés, Rossini, Monteverde (sic), Carissimi, Palestrina, Guido d'Arezzo, St Ambrose, Corneille, Molière, Cervantes, Virgil, Dante, Pythagoras,

Homer, Chaucer, Shakespeare, Milton, Goethe, Schiller, Bach, Gluck, Handel, Mozart, Mendelssohn, Haydn, Weber, Beethoven, Tallis, Gibbons, Lawes, Purcell, Arne, Boyce and Sir Henry Rowley Bishop. *Handbook*, pp. 34–46.

16. RA Add. H2/1228.
17. RA Add. H2/1266; H. H. Armstead, Royal Academy red scrap book.
18. RA Add. H2/1893.
19. RA Add. H2/1383.
20. RA Add. H2/1893.
21. RA Add. H2/1895.
22. The complete complement of Painters is: Turner, Wilkie, Reynolds, Gainsborough, Hogarth, Rembrandt, Rubens, Holbein, Dürer, Hubert and John (sic) van Eyck, Stephen of Cologne, Cimabue, Orcagna, Giotto, Fra Angelico, Ghirlandaio, Massicio, Leonardo, Raphael, Michael Angelo, Giovanni Bellini, Titian, Mantegna, Veronese, Tintoretto, Corregio, Annibale Carracci, Ludovico Carracci, Velasquez, Murillo, Poussin, Claude, David, Gévard, Géricault, Delacroix, Vernet, Delaroche, Ingres and Decamps. *Handbook*, pp. 46–60; RA Add. H2/1592–6.
23. RA Add. H2/2344.
24. RA Add. H2/1383–4.
25. RA Add. H2/1384.
26. Ibid.
27. The complete complement of Architects is: Pugin, Scott, Lockerelli, Ch. Barry, Chambers, Vanbrugh, Wren, Inigo Jones, Mansart, John Thorpe, Palladio, Vignola, Delorme, Sansovino, San Gallo, Peruzzi, Bramante, Wm. of Wykeham, Alberti, Brumelleschi, Giotto, Arnolfo di Lapo, Erwin von Steinbach, Jehan de Chelles, Robert de Loucy, William of Sens, William the Englishman, Abbé Juger, Anthemius, Apollodorus, Hermodorus, Callimachus, Libon, Callicrates, Ictinus, Muesicles, Chersiphron, Metageves, Rhoecus, Theodorus, Hiram, Bezaleel, Sennacherib, Nitocris and Cheeps. *Handbook*, pp. 60–72; RA Add. H2/1592–6.
28. RA Add. H4/40.
29. RA Add. H2/2139.
30. RA Add. H2/2140.
31. RA Add. H2/2141.
32. Ibid.
33. RA Add. H2/3161.
34. *The Builder*, vol. 30, 27 July 1872, p. 583.
35. The complete complement of Sculptors is: Egyptian, Assyrian (anonymous types, these), Rhoecus, Dibutades, Bupalus, Phidias, Scopas, Bruaxis, Leochares, Praxiteles, Lysippus, Chaves, Giulianodi Ravenna, Niccola Pisano, Lorenzo

Ghiberti, Luca della Robbia, William Torel, William of Ireland, Verrocchio, Donatello, Michael Angelo, Torrigiano, Giovanni di Bologna, Peter Vischer, Bandinelli, Cellini, Baccio d'Agnolo, Jean Goujon, Bernard Palissy, Pierre Bontemps, Germain Pilon, Alonzo Cano, Nicholas Stone, Bernini, Cibber, Pierre Puget, Grinling Gibbons, Francis Bird, John Bushnell, Roubiliac, Canova, Flaxman, David d'Angers and Thorwaldsen. *Handbook*, pp. 72–84; RA Add. H2/1592–6.

36. RA Add. H2/1229.
37. RA Add. H2/1580.
38. RA Add. H2/2254–9.
39. RA Add. H2/3154.
40. Ibid.
41. RA Add. H2/3539.
42. RA Add. H2/2628.
43. RA Add. H2/3629.
44. RA Add. H2/2941.
45. RA Add. H2/2996.
46. RA Add. H2/2944.
47. RA Add. H2/2973.
48. RA Add. H2/3013.
49. RA Add. H2/3015.
50. Ibid.
51. RA Add. H2/3091.

Chapter 7 : Skills

1. RA Add. H2/823.
2. RA Add. H2/960.
3. *Handbook*, pp. 31–2.
4. Rupert Gunnis, *Dictionary of British Sculptors*, revised edition, The Abbey Library, n.d., p. 393.
5. Ibid., pp. 418–20.
6. Walter G. Strickland, *Dictionary of Irish Artists*, Mansel and Company, Dublin & London, 1913, pp. 8–9.
7. RA Add. H2/834, 836, 837, 840, 842, 844.
8. RA Add. H2/837, 840.
9. RA Add. H2/921.
10. RA Add. H2/924.
11. RA Add. H2/925.
12. RA Add. H2/961.
13. RA Add. H2/928.
14. RA Add. H2/971–3.
15. RA Add. H2/973.
16. RA Add. H2/975.
17. RA Add. H2/944.
18. Ibid.
19. RA Add. H2/960–1.
20. RA Add. H2/961.
21. RA Add. H2/962, 954.
22. RA Add. H2/1079.

23. Ibid.
24. Ibid.
25. RA Add. H2/1080.
26. RA Add. H2/1080–1.
27. RA Add. H2/1074–5.
28. RA Add. H2/1899.
29. RA Add. H2/2216.
30. RA Add. H2/2959.
31. RA Add. H2/2983, 2991.
32. RA Add. H2/3286.
33. *Handbook*, p. 32.
34. RA Add. H2/3286.
35. RA Add. H2/3105.
36. RA Add. H2/3109.
37. RA Add. H4/n.p.
38. Ibid.
39. See *Handbook*, p. 32.
40. RA Add. H2/3104.
41. RA Add. H4/n.p.; *Handbook*, p. 31.
42. Gunnis, op. cit., p. 256.
43. RA Add. H4/n.p.; *Handbook*, p. 31.

Chapter 8: Continents
1. RA Add. H2/1079.
2. RA Add. H2/26.
3. H. H. Armstead, Royal Academy Scrapbooks, Diploma Works, vol. 1; Rupert Gunnis, op cit., pp. 249–50; Redgrave, op. cit., pp. 280–1.
4. Gunnis, pp. 153–4; Redgrave, pp. 156–7.
5. Gunnis, pp. 48–9. John Bell was apparently an unpopular sculptor. He had, as we have seen, a continuing interest in obelisks: *The Art Journal* of 1861 commenting 'Mr John Bell, who has been eagerly and rather unnaturally striving to erect an obelisk somewhere, is at length to be gratified We are not sorry to say it will be placed far off, at Bermuda ' p. 30 In February 1871, Bell complained of being cut dead by the Director of The British Museum, RA Add. H2/3331.
6. RA Add. H2/830.
7. RA Add. H2/871.
8. RA Add. H2/830–1.
9. RA Add. H2/830–1.
10. RA Add. H2/871.
11. RA Add. H2/887.
12. This conceit was employed also by H. H. Armstead in an unexecuted series of models for the lower groups which, never mentioned in any of the official correspondence preserved in the Royal Archives, exist in photographs preserved in the Royal Academy Library.
13. RA Add. H2/907.
14. *Handbook*, p. 28.

15. RA Add. H2/910.
16. RA Add. H2/944.
17. Ibid.
18. *Handbook*, p. 27.
19. RA Add. H2/911, 944.
20. RA Add. H2/914.
21. Armstead's own models of the continents, preserved in the Royal Academy photographs, also employ a lion as the colossal beast representative of Africa.
22. RA Add. H2/914.
23. RA Add. H2/1728.
24. RA Add. H2/917–18.
25. Ibid.
26. John Bell's America was published in *The Daily Telegraph*, 8 October 1861, *The Times*, 2 July 1872 and *The Pall Mall Gazette*, 14 July 1869.
27. RA Add. H2/944.
28. Ibid.
29. Ibid.
30. RA Add. H2/956.
31. RA Add. H2/965.
32. RA Add. H2/957.
33. RA Add. H2/958.
34. RA Add. H2/959.
35. RA Add. H2/968.
36. RA Add. H2/969.
37. RA Add. H2/970.
38. RA Add. H2/983.
39. RA Add. H2/1016–18.
40. RA Add. H2/1016, 1027.
41. RA Add. H2/1028.
42. RA Add. H2/1039.
43. RA Add. H2/1074–5.
44. RA Add. H2/1089–90.
45. *The Athenaeum*, 18 March 1865.
46. RA Add. H2/1094.
47. RA Add. H2/1432.
48. RA Add. H2/2539.
49. RA Add. H2/2543.
50. RA Add. H2/1432.
51. *Handbook*, pp. 28–9.
52. Ibid.
53. Ibid.
54. RA Add. H2/3716, 3719.

Chapter 9: The Higher Life and Soul of the Memorial
1. RA Add. H11/7178.
2. RA Add. H4/21.
3. RA Add. H4/22.
4. *Handbook*, p. 21.
5. RA Add. H4/27.
6. Ibid., 21–2. The angels were in gilded bronze, designed by J. B. Philip and executed by Messrs

Skidmore.
7. RA Add. H2/889.
8. *The Builder*, 11 May 1862, p. 357; A. H. Layard, 'Paper on Mosaic Decoration' read before the RIBA, revised by the author and reprinted for the Venice and Murano Glass Company, London, n.d. (but before 1872), pp. 17–18.
9. RA Add. H2/1411.
10. RA Add. H2/1412.
11. RA Add. H2/889.
12. Ibid.
13. RA Add. H2/890b; RA Add. H2/1203–4.
14. RA Add. H2/1495.
15. Layard, op. cit.; *Handbook*, p. 23.
16. Layard, op. cit.; RA Add. H4/16.
17. RA Add. H2/1852–3, 1855, 1857.
18. RA Add. H2/1847, 1851.
19. Ibid.
20. RA Add. H2/1900.
21. RA Add. H2/2875–7. The suggested Latin inscription was to be the Eulogy of Pompey by Cato in Lucan, ix. Grey had to take advice on this (being a cautious scholar), and was astonished to find how inappropriate the setting was, the preceding lines being 'casta domus, luxusque carens, corruptaque [nunquam] Fortuna dominum'.
22. RA Add. H2/2890.
23. RA Add. H2/2909.
24. RA Add. H2/2911, 2913, 2914, 2916.
25. *Handbook*, p. 24.
26. Algernon Graves, *Royal Academy Exhibitors*, Henry Graves and George Bell, 1905, vol. I, p. 62.
27. *Handbook*, p. 24.
28. Ibid.; *The Pall Mall Gazette*, 14 July 1869.
29. Ibid.
30. *Handbook*, pp. 24–5.
31. *Handbook*, pp. 25–6.
32. *The Pall Mall Gazette*, loc. cit.
33. RA Add. H4/13.
34. Ibid.
35. RA Add. H4/17. The figures '21' and '360' were later pencil additions to the manuscript, suggesting some investigative procedures had taken place before any commitment was made!
36. Charles Boutell, 'The Metal Work of the Memorial', *Art Journal*, January, 1867, pp. 13–15.
37. Ibid.
38. RA Add. H4/24.
39. RA Add. H4/25.
40. RA Add. H4/18.

Chapter 10: Flowers, Fashion and Sunshine
1. RA Add. H4/8.

2. *The Builder*, vol. 24, 14 May 1866.
3. RA Add. H2/860.
4. Ibid.
5. RA Add. H2/980.
6. RA Add. H2/1042.
7. RA Add. H2/1056. See also Gavin Stamp, 'Sir Gilbert Scott's Recollections', *Architectural History*, vol. 19. 1976, pp. 54–73.
8. RA Add. H2/1275.
9. RA Add. H4/2.
10. RA Add. H4/34–5.
11. RA Add. H2/1799; *Building News*, 12 April 1867.
12. *Journal of the Royal Society of Arts*, 4 April 1870; RA Add. H2/3195–6.
13. RA Add. H4/3212.
14. *The Standard*, 20 May 1870.
15. *The Times*, 25 May 1870. However, the *Times'* correspondent did not know that the proposal to straighten the road in fact dated back to the original Architects' Report of 1862.
16. *The Daily News*, 31 May 1870. For instance, *The Saturday Review* for 11 June 1870 pointed out that the Commissioners of the 1851 Exhibition had been sold land at about one twenty-fifth of its true value.
17. *The Echo*, 31 May 1870.
18. *The Saturday Review*, 11 June 1870.
19. *The Daily Telegraph*, 16 June 1870.
20. RA Add. H2/3243.
21. RA Add. H2/3274.
22. Ibid.
23. RA Add. H2/3423.
24. RA Add. H2/3421.
25. Scott's identifying 'Epsilon' with John Bell would seem to be convincing. In its issue of 28 April 1871, the *Journal of the Royal Society of Arts* published a letter of 'Epsilon's' which exactly repeats ideas already popularly established as Bell's.
26. RA Add. H2/3047–50.
27. Ibid.
28. RA Add. H2/3690.
29. Queen Victoria's *Journal*, 1 July 1872.
30. Ibid.
31. RA Add. H2/3812.
32. RA Add. H2/3822.
33. RA Add. H2/3849.
34. RA Add. H2/4606–7.
35. RA Add. H2/3763.
36. RA Add. H2/3767b.
37. RA Add. H2/3765; it was after Cole's suggestion that Kelk had, in any case, offered his services at cost, RA Add. H2/472.
38. RA Add. H2/3767c.
39. Ibid. Further correspondence in the Royal Archives

does, indeed, suggest that Kelk was displeased by
being offered only a knighthood, RA Add. H2/
3797–8.

40. *Architectural Journal*, May 1871.
41. A vast selection of contemporary cuttings is
preserved in RA Add. H2/4000.
42. Martin Shaw Briggs, op. cit.
43. Rupert Gunnis, *A Dictionary of British Sculpture*,
The Abbey Press, n.d., p. 153.
44. This information was offered by Celia Crampton.
45. Charles Handley-Read, 'The Albert Memorial
Re-Assessed', *Country Life*, 14 December 1961,
pp. 1514–16.
46. Stephen Potter, *The Muse in Chains*, Cape, 1937,
pp. 126–39.
I am grateful to Ian Gregor for this reference.
47. Hermione Gingold broadcast her 'Desert Island
Discs' on 18 August 1969.
48. Eugène-Emmanuel Viollet-le-Duc, 'French Reports
on the International Exhibition of 1871', *JSA*,
19 July 1872, pp. 721–2.
49. *The Builder*, 27 July 1873.
50. Edmund Gosse, 'The Future of Sculpture in
London', *The Magazine of Art*, 1881, p. 281.
51. Quoted in Charles Handley-Read, op. cit.
52. Lytton Strachey, *Queen Victoria*, Chatto, 1921,
pp. 234–9.
53. R. G. Collingwood, *An Autobiography*, Oxford
University Press, 1939, p. 29.
54. Sir Gilbert Scott died in 1878.
55. *Recollections*, p. 225.
56. RA Add. H2/544.

Index